Shape Up Your Fat Quarters

by Debbie Caffrey

Debbie's Creative Moments, Inc.
P.O. Box 29418
Santa Fe, NM 87592-9418

www.debbiescreativemoments.com

Credits

Illustrated by

Debbie Caffrey

Photographed by

Pat Berrett
Albuquerque, New Mexico

Printed by

Palmer Printing
St. Cloud, Minnesota

Proofread by

Erin Caffrey

Thank You to

E. E. Schenck
Portland, Oregon
Provided Maywood Fabrics for
Hot Apple Cider

Shape Up Your Fat Quarters

©2002 by Debbie Caffrey

Published by

Debbie's Creative Moments, Inc.
P. O. Box 29418
Santa Fe, NM 87592-9418
USA

ISBN: 0-9645777-6-3

First Printing, 2002

Table of Contents

Introduction

What are fat quarters?

Most quilters, when they hear "fat quarters", do not think about body type. A fat quarter is a specific cut of fabric.

A true quarter yard of fabric is 9" of fabric cut from the bolt, selvage to selvage. The true quarter yard measures approximately 9" x 42". A fat quarter is equivalent in area to a true quarter yard, but it is in a much more usable shape for most projects. A fat quarter is 18" of fabric, a half yard, which is then cut in half on the fold. This results in a piece of fabric that is approximately 18" x 21".

Fat quarters have become very popular in most quilt shops. Shops have creatively coordinated, folded, and packaged them to tempt the impulse buyers and fabric collectors.

So, *you* fit into one of those two categories! Well, I do, too. Once I get past the beautiful packaging I begin to think about how to use those fabulous fabrics in a quilt. It can be a challenging task for some. How many fat quarters are needed for the quilt? Will I efficiently use the fat quarters, or will I be left with large amounts of scraps?

Some quilt patterns suggest fat quarters as the amount of fabric to purchase, but they do not give specific cutting instructions for the use of fat quarters. The patterns in this book are written specifically for fat quarters. With that in mind, they are designed to efficiently use the entire piece with very little waste in most cases. Conversely, because there is so little fabric left, there is no room for cutting errors!

What happens if you do make a cutting error? Grab another fat quarter and keep cutting. Does it matter if your quilt has seventeen different fabrics instead of sixteen? Of course not.

Advantages of Using Fat Quarters

Using fat quarters speeds the cutting of multiple fabric quilts. Fat quarters are fairly uniform in size. Therefore, they can be neatly stacked to cut through layers. I have yet to hear someone in one of my classes exclaim, *"Rotary cutting is my favorite part of quilting!"*. Most of us agree that rotary cutting is a way to speed along the mundane task of cutting many pieces.

Less fabric is wasted in the process of squaring up fat quarters. Squaring up any piece of fabric from selvage to selvage after it has been prewashed will often waste several inches of fabric or more. That is a large portion of a true quarter yard of fabric.

It is easy to change the sizes of quilts made with fat quarters. If you want a larger quilt, use more fat quarters. Similarly, use fewer fat quarters to make a smaller quilt.

Using Scraps and Larger Yardage

The quilts in this book can be made with fewer fabrics than suggested, or they can be made with many more. Examples of these extremes are the *Two Color Snail's Trail* on page 17 and *Gwen & Friends* on page 25.

General Instructions

It is very important to take the time to review the general instructions prior to using the patterns. Many of the questions that can arise by going directly to the construction of the quilts will be answered in this chapter.

Similarly, read the pattern before beginning to cut. Becoming familiar with the pattern will help you avoid mistakes.

Fabric Yardage & Preparation

Except for the fat quarters, which rarely have much excess, the other fabric yardage is fairly generous, allowing for shrinkage, straightening, and minor errors.

I prefer to wash and press my fabrics prior to using them. I began this habit when I first started quilting. I continue to wash them because I do not care to use washed and unwashed fabrics together in the same project. I have made quilts using only new, unwashed fabric, and I did not like handling the fabrics.

To avoid distorting your fabric as you press the yardage, move your iron in strokes which are parallel to the selvages. That is in the direction of the stable warp yarns which will not stretch as you press. I often have quilters come to class with fabrics which seem to have wavy, wobbly edges along the selvages. Usually this problem is not due to the quality of the fabric. It is created by moving the iron from side to side between the selvages while applying any combination of the following: heavy pressure, steam, and starch or sizing.

Steam, starch, and sizing are fine, but take care that you do not distort the fabric. Some patterns will require you to sew along the bias edges of triangles and trapezoids. Spray starching your fabrics prior to cutting them will help stabilize them against stretching as you sew.

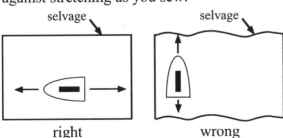

right   wrong

Cutting

Some patterns in this book require cutting fabric yardage. An example is the background fabric for *Scrappy and Sensational*. In such cases, cut strips across the width of fabric. The strips will be approximately 42" long with selvages on the two short ends.

You may choose to work with odds and ends of fabric from your stash that are not fat quarters. If these pieces are large enough, make a fat quarter from them to streamline your cutting.

Set aside any pieces that you are using that cannot be cut into a fat quarter, such as scraps and true quarter yard pieces, and cut them separately.

Cutting the Fat Quarters

I feel comfortable cutting through eight layers of fabric at one time. You will need to use the medium (45 mm) or large (60 mm) rotary cutter for cutting many layers.

STEP 1

Stack the fat quarters that will be cut into the same number and sizes of pieces in the following way (See photo 1 below.):

open to a single layer,
right side up,
selvages aligned atop one another at the left,
top edges as even as possible, and
smallest piece on top.

photo 1

STEP 2

Before making the first cut, read the cutting instructions to determine which way the fat quarters are to be cut into strips. Sometimes they are cut *parallel to* the selvages, as shown in photos 2, 3, and 4. At other times, they are cut into strips in the direction that is *perpendicular to* the selvages, as shown in photo 5.

The initial strip cutting direction is extremely important because the fat quarters are not square. There usually is not enough fabric to cut all the pieces if the strips are not first cut in the correct direction. Some patterns use both directions. For example, the light fat quarters may be cut in a perpendicular direction while the dark fat quarters are cut parallel to the selvages.

STEP 3

Trimming all four sides may leave you short of fabric. If you are cutting *parallel to the selvage, remove the selvage edge*. If you are cutting *perpendicular to the selvage, trim the top edge of the fat quarters* so that it is even and forms a ninety degree angle with the selvage. Straighten and square only the one edge of the stack of fat quarters. Then, cut the required number and sizes of strips (photos 4 and 5).

NOTE: When cutting wide strips, use two rulers or one large square. Photos 2 and 3 show how to use a large square. Begin cutting at the bottom edge. Slide the square up to the top of the fat quarters (photo 3) and complete the cut.

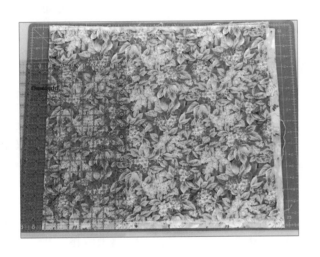

photo 2

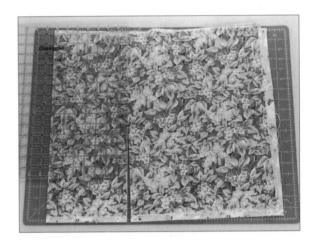

photo 3

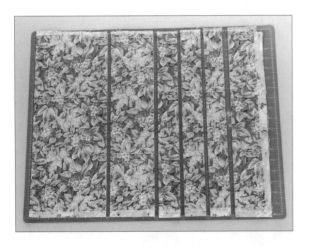

photo 4

photo 5

STEP 4

Continue cutting the fabrics as directed. Crosscut the strips into the required squares or rectangles (photo 6). Some strips will not be cut until after they are used for strip piecing.

Then, cut the squares into half-square or quarter-square triangles if directed by the pattern.

Occasionally, a strip will be used to cut more than one size of square. For example, the *Hot Apple Cider* pattern requires two 4 1/4" strips. One strip is cut into four 4 1/4" squares. From the second strip you cut two more 4 1/4" squares. Then, the remainder of that second strip is trimmed to 3 1/2" wide and cut into three 3 1/2" squares. See photo 7.

Finally, if you are making *Hot Apple Cider* or *Scrappy and Sensational*, cut trapezoids from the strips. Detailed instructions and photos for this procedure are included in those patterns' instructions.

Using the Templates

When using templates, I use a copy machine or my computer to make templates. *Be sure to compare copies to the original! Many copiers greatly distort the image and the templates may be incorrect.*

Tape the templates to the underside of any suitable tool using double sided tape. See photos 8 and 9. I prefer to use a temporary adhesive. Look for it at your local craft or office supply store.

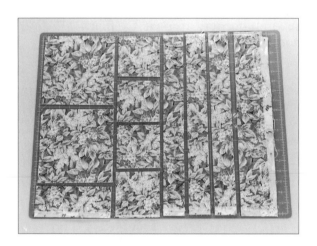

photo 6

photo 7

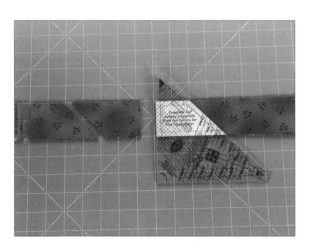

photo 8

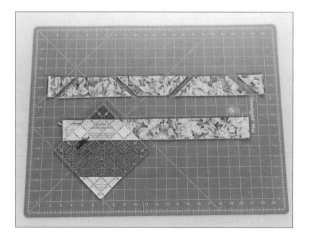

photo 9

9

Sewing Precision

The success of your quilts depends upon precise seam allowances. ***I cannot stress this point enough.*** Do not believe the person who tells you that as long as you are consistent, it will be okay. Most quilts have areas of many seams as well as other areas with few seams. They must be constructed with accurate seam allowances. If you have not checked your seam allowances in the past, do so by performing the following test.

TEST: From scraps cut four rectangles that measure 1 1/2" x 4 1/2". Sew them together along the long edges using a scant 1/4" seam allowance. That is about a needle's width narrower than a true 1/4".

Press the seam allowances to one side. The finished piece should measure 4 1/2" square. If not, adjust your seam allowance and repeat the test.

The finished sample will measure 4 1/2" square.

Borders

The outer border strips should be cut with the lengthwise grain in the long direction whenever possible. Cutting them in this direction will keep the borders from stretching and rippling. The yardage requirements allow for lengthwise grain borders. It is not necessary that narrow inner borders be cut along the lengthwise grain.

My solution for cutting accurate, long, lengthwise grain border strips is summed up in one word -- tear. Tearing is only recommended for 100 per cent cotton fabrics. Test fabrics of other fiber content before tearing the yardage.

Fabrics are woven with the strong warp yarns running in the lengthwise direction and the weaker weft yarns in the crosswise direction. Because of that, the fabric doesn't stretch along the lengthwise grain while having a good deal of give on the crosswise grain. When tearing across the width of fabrics, you are breaking the stronger yarns, which leads to snags and weakening of the fabric beyond the 1/4" seam allowances.

On the other hand, when tearing fabric along its length, you are breaking the weak yarns and tearing between and parallel to the warp yarns. The result is a much smoother edge and a perfectly straight, on-grain border strip.

If you are unsure about how well your fabric will tear, start by tearing off a selvage. Clip one end of the fabric about 1" away from the selvage edge. Tear this selvage off. Do not be timid. Pull firmly and rather quickly. What do you think of the edge? Press the torn edge. How does it look now? If it is satisfactory, you are ready to tear the borders.

Lay an end of the border fabric flat on a table. Measure the desired cut width of your border from the edge where you have removed the selvage. Make a clip at this point on the end of the fabric just as you did when removing the selvage. Measure from this first clip and make a second clip for the second border. Repeat to mark all four borders. See the drawing below. Tear!

Press the border strips. Since I prewash my fabrics before making a quilt, I do not press the border fabric until it is torn into strips. A narrow strip of fabric is easier to press than yards of the full width fabric.

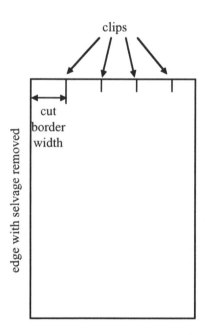

clips

cut border width

edge with selvage removed

Measuring and easing are important steps. Your quilt may not be square if you eliminate these steps. Be sure the quilt is pressed well before measuring it. As you are measuring, keep the quilt top fairly taut on a flat surface. The quilt top contains many seams, and they each have a slight amount of slack where the seam allowances are pressed to the side. Conversely, the borders have few or no seams and are cut along the stable, lengthwise grain. Therefore, keeping the quilt taut while measuring is imperative, but do not stretch quilts that are set on point.

Borders can be applied with either overlapped or mitered corners. The yardage allowed in this book is for overlapped borders. None of the quilts was completed with mitered corners. However, if you choose to miter the corners, purchase an additional half yard of border fabric to allow for the extra length required for mitering.

Overlapped Corners

Follow these instructions for adding borders with overlapped corners. Find the length of the quilt. Measure in several places to determine the average length. Take measurements along seam lines and in areas that go through the centers of the blocks, but not along the outside edges. Cut two border strips 1/2” wider than the desired finished width of the border. Trim the length of the borders to the average measured length of the quilt.

Pin the borders to the sides of the quilt, matching the center points and ends of the quilt and borders. Continue pinning the borders to the quilt, easing if necessary. Sew. Press the seam allowances toward the borders.

Now, determine the width of the quilt, measuring in several places, as before. Include the additional width created by the side borders. Cut two border strips to fit (finished border width plus 1/2” x width of quilt) and pin them to the top and bottom of the quilt as you did the side borders. Sew. Press the seam allowances toward the borders. See the drawing at the right.

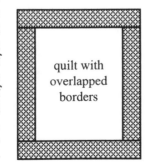

quilt with overlapped borders

If you are adding more than one border, repeat the above steps for each border.

Quilting and Binding

There are books and classes devoted solely to quilting and binding. Almost every quilting magazine on the market contains basic instruction for quilting and binding in each issue. Quilting and binding are highly visible and are a part of every quilt. Learn to do them well. Take advantage of demonstrations and classes that are available to you.

Happy Endings, written by Mimi Dietrich and published by That Patchwork Place, is a good reference for additional information on binding.

After quilting, trim the excess batting and backing in preparation for binding. I use a 1/2” wide binding. Some quilts have pieced edges, and therefore, have only 1/4” seam allowances. To allow for the 1/2” binding, leave an additional 1/4” of backing and batting beyond the quilt top when trimming the excess. This will create the necessary 1/2” seam allowance.

For a 1/2” double binding, cut cross-grain strips 3 1/4” wide. Bias strips are only necessary for binding curves, although, some fabrics, like plaids and stripes, make a more interesting binding when cut on the bias. Cut enough strips to go around the perimeter of your quilt. Sew the strips together, end on end, and press the seam allowances open. Press the binding in half, wrong sides together, lengthwise.

Sew the binding to the quilt with 1/2” seam allowances, aligning the raw edges of the binding with the cut edge of the quilt. Start in the middle of one side, *leaving the first six inches of binding unsewn*. Stitch, stopping 1/2” from the corner. Lift your presser foot and pull the quilt out a few inches from under the machine to fold the binding. It is not necessary to clip the threads now. Rotate the quilt a quarter turn, counterclockwise. Fold the binding up and away, creating a 45 degree angle to the corner. Then, fold the binding back down toward you.

Begin stitching at the edge of the quilt. Continue stitching down the second side, stopping 1/2” from the corner. Miter this corner as you did the first one and continue around the quilt. After you have mitered the last corner, *stop stitching 12" from where you first began to attach the binding*.

Trim the excess binding, leaving 1/4" extra on each end for seam allowances. Stitch the two ends of the binding together. Press the seam allowances open. Finish stitching this section of the binding to the quilt.

Push the binding to the back of the quilt and pin in place. The folded edge of the binding should just cover the stitching line. Fold the corners into neat miters on the back of the quilt. Hand stitch the binding into place.

Gwen & Friends

The size of the quilt shown on page 25 is 85 1/2" x 103 1/2", a queen size.

This quilt was made in memory of a dear friend, Gwen Glueck of Portland, Oregon. Gwen, her daughter Arlene, and many friends attended numerous quilting retreats and conferences with me in Bend, Oregon, and at Diamond Lake, Oregon. We lost Gwen to a sudden heart attack in November of 1999. It was hard, but Arlene was able to come to the fall 2000 retreat without her mother. She brought along a bit of Gwen's fabric stash. Everyone at the retreat used some of Gwen's fabric and added her own to make a number of nine patch and half-square triangle blocks. We told Arlene I wanted help making a quilt for my book and that sharing Gwen's fabric would be a way that her mother could be a part of it, too. The quilt was presented to a surprised and very happy Arlene the following fall.

Fabric Requirements

Twenty-four light fat quarters	
Thirty dark fat quarters	
Binding	**1 yard**
Backing	**8 yards**

Cutting

Light Fat Quarters

Stack the fat quarters as directed in the general directions. Make three stacks of eight fabrics.

Cut strips *perpendicular to* the selvages as shown in figure 1 on the following page.

Cut two strips 5 3/8" wide from each fabric.
    From these strips cut a total of four 5 3/8" squares of each fabric.
        Cut the 5 3/8" squares once, diagonally, to make two half-square triangles
        from each square.   Yield: 8 triangles of each fabric

Cut three strips 2" wide from each fabric.

Dark Fat Quarters

Stack *twenty-four* of the thirty fat quarters into three stacks of eight fabrics. Reserve the other six for later cutting.

Cut strips *perpendicular to* the selvages as shown in figure 2 on the following page.

Cut one strip 5 3/8" wide from each of the twenty-four fabrics.
    From this strip cut a total of three 5 3/8" squares of each fabric.
        Cut the 5 3/8" squares once, diagonally, to make two half-square triangles
        from each square.   Yield: 6 triangles of each fabric

Dark Fat Quarters, Continued (the first twenty-four fat quarters)

Cut one strip 5" wide from each of the twenty-four fabrics.
    From this strip cut a total of four 5" squares of each fabric.

Cut three strips 2" wide from each of the twenty-four fabrics.

Remaining Six Dark Fat Quarters

Stack the remaining fat quarters as directed in the general directions.

Cut off the selvages and cut strips *parallel to* the selvages as shown in figure 3.

Cut three strips 5 3/8" wide from each of the six fabrics.
    From these three strips cut a total of nine 5 3/8" squares of each fabric.
        Cut the 5 3/8" squares once, diagonally, to make two half-square triangles
        from each square.   Yield: 18 triangles of each fabric

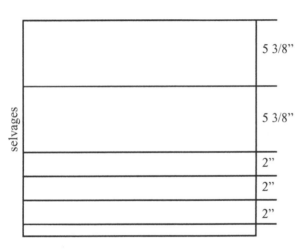

fig. 1

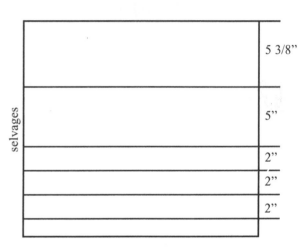

fig. 2

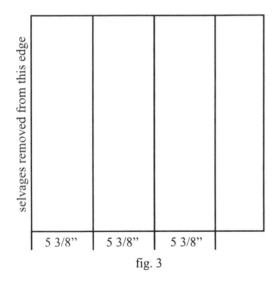

fig. 3

Piecing

Make half-square triangle blocks using the fabrics randomly. Make thirty-seven blocks that use two different dark triangles. Make 178 blocks that use one light triangle and one dark triangle. There will be a few light triangles left over. These triangles will not be used to complete the quilt.

Press the seam allowances toward the darker triangle. Trim the dog ears.

make 37

make 178

Use all three 2" wide strips of one dark fabric and all three 2" wide strips of one light fabric to make the panels shown below. Press the seam allowances in the directions shown by the arrows.

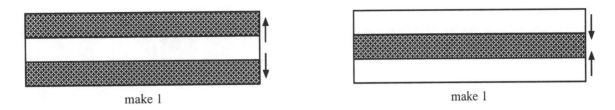

make 1   make 1

Crosscut nine 2" wide sections from each of the panels.

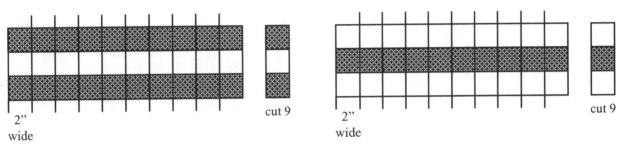

2"   cut 9   2"   cut 9
wide   wide

Sew these sections together to make three of each of the nine patch blocks shown at the right.

Press the seam allowances in the directions shown by the arrows.

Repeat the above steps with the remaining 2" wide strips to make a total of 142 nine patch blocks, seventy-one with dark corners and seventy-one with light corners.

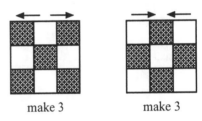

make 3   make 3

Completing the Quilt Top

Arrange the pieced blocks as shown on the following page. Only a few fill patterns have been used in the graphic to show where the lights and darks are positioned. Place the 5" squares around the perimeter of the quilt. There will be sixteen 5" squares left over and not used to complete the quilt.

Sew the blocks into horizontal rows. Press the seam allowances toward the nine patches. Following the same pressing pattern, press the blocks on the ends of the rows so that they will oppose those in the next row. Sew the rows together. Press the seam allowances to one side.

Options to Consider

Look at the illustration on the following page. It looks like the quilt has sashing between the blocks. Cut the sashes 1" wide (They will finish to 1/2" wide.) to make your finished quilt with a grid work on the surface.

Turn the blocks on point to achieve vertical or horizontal bands of light and dark.

Try other settings like barn raising, zig zag, spiral, or random weaving trails.

Layout of *Gwen & Friends*

Due to space limitations, the illustration below does not show the squares around the perimeter.
Before sewing the top together, place the 5" squares of dark around the edges of the quilt.

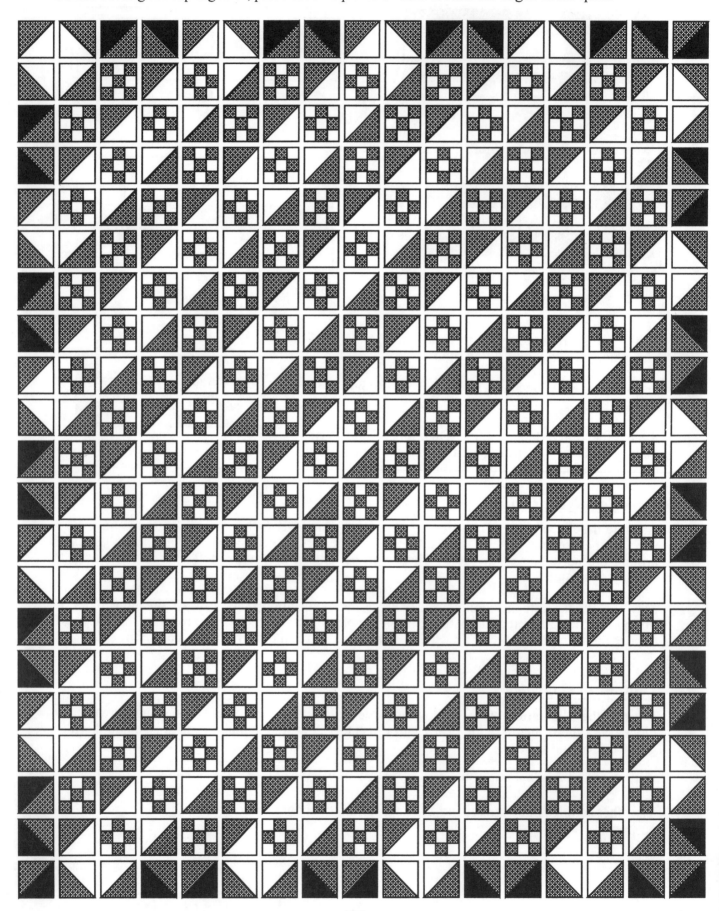

Two Fabric Snail's Trail -- 42" x 54"

Pieced and Machine Quilted by Debbie Caffrey of Santa Fe, New Mexico

17

Homespun Snail's Trail -- 66" x 86"

Pieced by Debbie Caffrey and Machine Quilted by Mary Johnson of Sutton, Alaska

Snails in the Garden -- 62" x 86"

Pieced by Debbie Caffrey and Machine Quilted by Melodye Livingston of Wasilla, Alaska

Rocky Mountain Puzzle -- 58 1/2" x 70"

Pieced by Debbie Caffrey and Machine Quilted by Phyllis Kent of Los Lunas, New Mexico

Hot Apple Cider -- 77 1/2" x 90 1/4"

Pieced by Debbie Caffrey and Machine Quilted by Phyllis Kent of Los Lunas, New Mexico

Confined to Quarters -- 63" x 72"

Pieced by Debbie Caffrey and Machine Quilted by Phyllis Kent of Los Lunas, New Mexico

Scrappy and Sensational -- 73" x 91"

Pieced by Debbie Caffrey and Machine Quilted by Karen Tomczak of Anchorage, Alaska

Ninety-Six Miles an Hour -- 64" x 88"

Pieced by Debbie Caffrey and Machine Quilted by Vel Saddington of Albuquerque, New Mexico

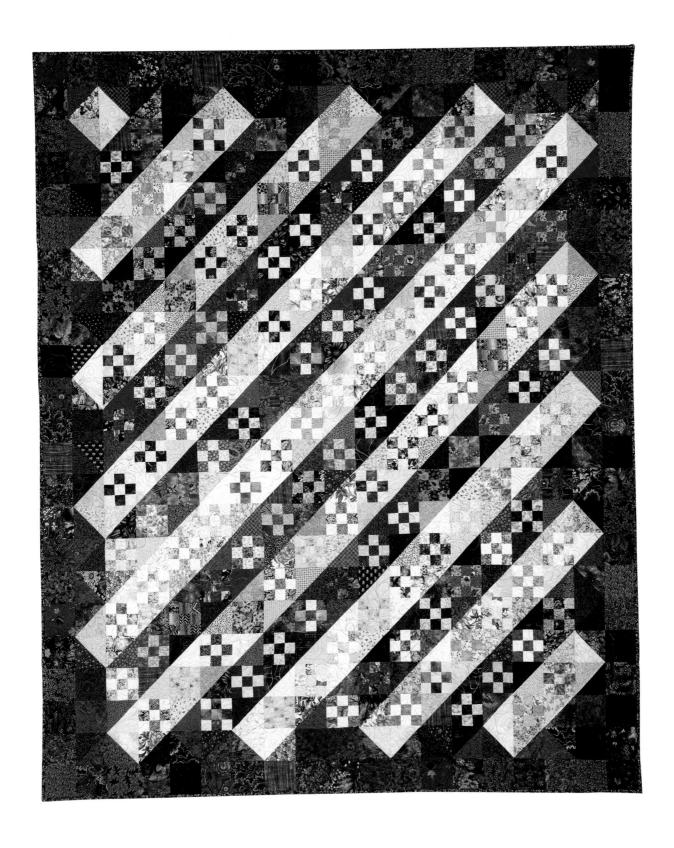

Gwen & Friends -- 85 1/2" x 103 1/2"

Group Quilt Pieced by Diamond Lake Fall Retreat 2000
and Machine Quilted by Crys Kyle of Bend, Oregon

25

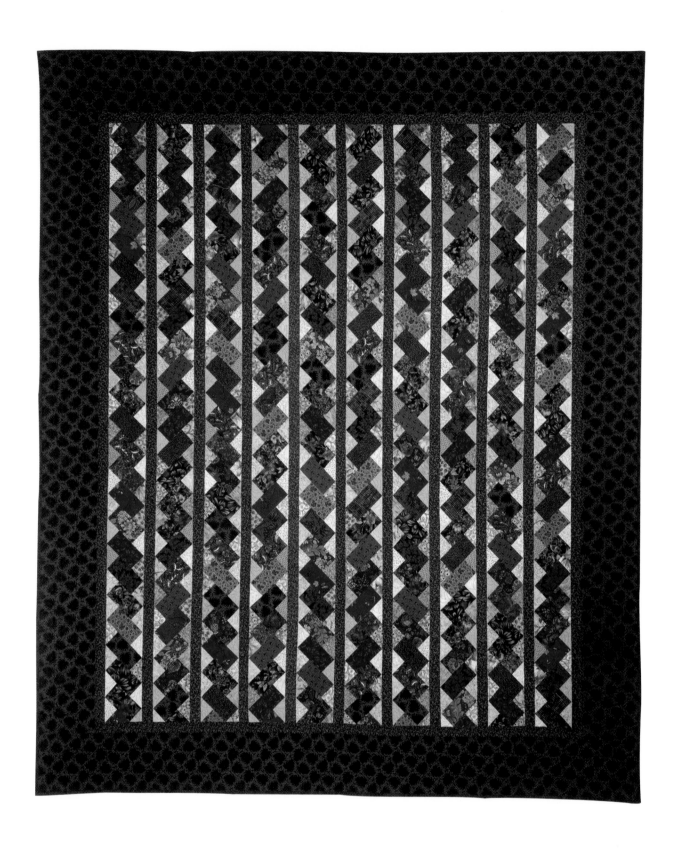

Stacked Bricks -- 86" x 103"

Pieced by Debbie Caffrey and Machine Quilted by Phyllis Kent of Los Lunas, New Mexico

Delectable Mountains -- 67" x 89 1/2"

Pieced by Debbie Caffrey and Machine Quilted by Vel Saddington of Albuquerque, New Mexico

Prints Charming -- 84" x 102"

Pieced by Debbie Caffrey and Machine Quilted by Phyllis Kent of Los Lunas, New Mexico

Prints Charming

The size of the quilt shown on page 28 is 84" x 102", a queen size.

Fabric Requirements

Fourteen light fat quarters

Fourteen medium-dark large scale print fat quarters

Fourteen dark tone on tone fat quarters

Border	**2 3/4 yards**
Binding	**1 yard**
Backing	**8 yards**

Cutting

Light Fat Quarters

Stack the fat quarters as directed in the general directions. Make two stacks of seven fabrics.

Cut strips *perpendicular to* the selvages as shown in figure 1.

Cut one strip 5 1/2" wide from each fabric.
　　From this strip cut a total of three 5 1/2" squares of each fabric.
　　　　Cut the 5 1/2" squares twice, diagonally, to make four quarter-square triangles
　　　　from each square.　　　　　　Yield: 12 triangles of each fabric

Cut two strips 3" wide from each fabric.
　　From these two strips cut a total of twelve 3" squares of each fabric.
　　　　Cut these squares once, diagonally, to make two half-square triangles from
　　each square.　　　　　　Yield: 24 triangles of each fabric

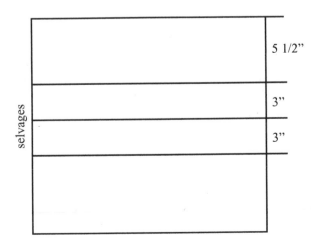

fig. 1

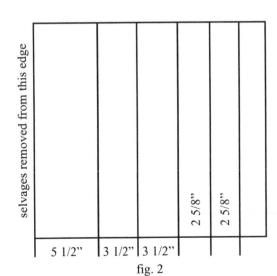

fig. 2

Medium-Dark Large Scale Print Fat Quarters

Stack the fat quarters as directed in the general directions. Make two stacks of seven fabrics.

Cut off the selvages and cut strips **parallel to** the selvages as shown in figure 2 on the previous page.

Cut one strip 5 1/2" wide from each fabric.
    From this strip cut a total of three 5 1/2" squares of each fabric.
        Cut the 5 1/2" squares twice, diagonally, to make four quarter-square triangles
        from each square.   Yield: 12 triangles of each fabric

Cut two strips 3 1/2" wide from each fabric.
    From these two strips cut a total of six 3 1/2" squares of each fabric.

Cut two strips 2 5/8" wide from each fabric.
    From these two strips cut a total of twelve 2 5/8" squares of each fabric.

Dark Tone on Tone Fat Quarters

Stack the fat quarters as directed in the general directions. Make two stacks of seven fabrics.

Cut off the selvages and cut strips **parallel to** the selvages as shown in figure 3.

Cut four strips 4 3/4" wide from each fabric.
    From these four strips cut a total of twenty-four 2 5/8" x 4 3/4" rectangles of each fabric.

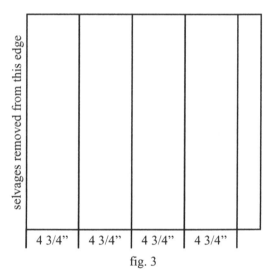

fig. 3

Piecing

Use the fabrics randomly throughout your piecing. To avoid confusion in the following directions, only one fill pattern is used for each value: light, medium-dark, and dark. Count and make only the number of units required in each step. There will be a few pieces of various sizes left over and not used to complete this quilt.

Sew a half-square triangle of light (those cut from the 3" squares) to two opposite sides of **eighty** 3 1/2" squares of the large scale medium-dark fabrics. There will be four squares left over. ***NOTE: Center the triangle with the square. The tips of the triangle will extend 3/8" beyond the square on both ends.*** Allow this to happen so that the pieces are positioned correctly for the next step. See figure 4. Press the seam allowances toward the triangles. Trim the dog ears.

make 80

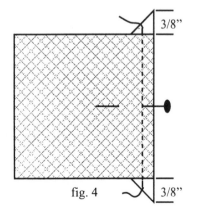

fig. 4

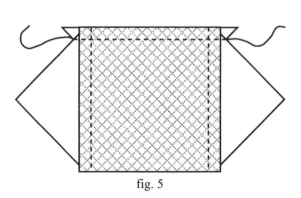

fig. 5

Sew a half-square triangle of light to the remaining two sides of the units you just completed to make eighty square within a square blocks. ***NOTE: This time the pieces will meet at the seam line.*** See figure 5 on the previous page.

make 80

Press the seam allowances toward the triangles that you just added. Trim the dog ears.

Set aside two light and two medium-dark quarter-square triangles (those cut from the 5 1/2" squares) for the corners of the quilt.

A - make 14

Sew fourteen light and fourteen medium-dark quarter-square triangles into pairs. Make sure the units look exactly like A when the units are finished. Press the seam allowances toward the medium-dark. Trim the dog ears. These units will be used along the top and bottom edges of the quilt.

Use the remaining quarter-square triangles of light and medium-dark to make 144 units like B. Press the seam allowances toward the medium-dark. Trim the dog ears.

B - make 144

Set aside eighteen of the B units you just completed. These units will be used along the sides of the quilt. Use the remaining 126 units to make sixty-three hourglass blocks. Press the seam allowances to one side. Trim the dog ears.

Use 126 B's to make 63 hourglass blocks.

Completing the Quilt Top

The 2 5/8" x 4 3/4" rectangles are the sashes, and the 2 5/8" squares are the cornerstones.

Cut one strip 4 1/4" wide from your border fabric.
    Cut this strip into nine 4 1/4" squares.
        Cut these squares twice, diagonally, to make four quarter-square triangles
        from each.   Yield: 36 triangles
        These triangles are placed on the ends of the sashing/cornerstone rows.

Arrange the blocks, the remaining A and B units, and the setting pieces in diagonal rows. Make sure the hourglass blocks are rotated into the correct position to complete the pattern. They should all be positioned in exactly the same way. A diagram of the quilt is on the following page. At the bottom of this page you will find an exploded view of the upper left corner of the quilt to get you started. Again, to avoid confusion, only one pattern is used for each value: light, medium-dark, and dark. The solid black triangles at the ends of the sashing/cornerstone rows are those that you just cut from the border fabric.

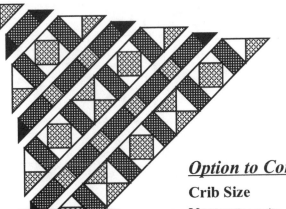

Piece the diagonal rows. Press the seam allowances toward the sashes in all rows. Sew the rows together. Press the seam allowances toward the sashing/cornerstone rows.

Add borders with overlapped corners. Cut the borders 6 1/2" wide to finish the quilt shown in the photo. See page 10 for more information on borders.

Option to Consider

Crib Size

Use scraps to make a crib size. Make twenty square within a square blocks, twelve hourglass blocks, six A units, eight B units, two light corners, two medium-dark corners, and eighteen side triangles of border fabric.

Layout for *Prints Charming*

The quilt is shown before the addition of borders. The upper left quarter, which is outlined in bold, shows the layout of the crib size quilt. Side triangles of border fabric should be placed where needed along the bottom and right edges to finish the crib size.

Homespun Snail's Trail

The size of the quilt shown on page 18 is 66" x 86", a twin size.

Fabric Requirements

Nine Homespun Plaid Fat Quarters
Use additional scraps or fat quarters for more variety of fabrics.

Light Homespun	**1 yard**
Sashing	**1 3/4 yards**
Border	**2 1/4 yards**
Binding	**7/8 yard**
Backing	**5 1/4 yards**

Cutting

Fat Quarters

Stack the fat quarters as directed in the general directions. Make two stacks: five fabrics in the first and four fabrics in the second.

Cut strips *perpendicular to* the selvages as shown in figure 1.

Cut two strips 4 7/8" wide from each fabric.
  From these two strips cut a total of eight 4 7/8" squares of each fabric.
    Cut these squares once, diagonally, to make two half-square triangles from each square.   Yield: 16 triangles of each fabric

Cut three strips 2 1/2" wide from each fabric.
  From these three strips cut a total of twenty-one 2 1/2" squares of each fabric.

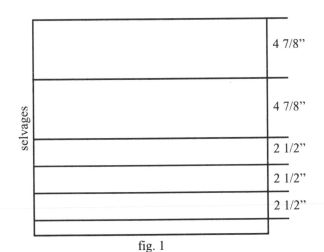

fig. 1

Light Homespun

Cut five strips 5 1/4" wide.
  Cut these strips into thirty-five 5 1/4" squares.
    Cut these squares twice, diagonally, to make four quarter-square triangles from each.
      Yield: 140 triangles

Piecing

Organize your pieces into thirty-five sets prior to sewing. Each set will make one block. Use four fabrics for each block. The pieces needed for one block are the following:

Homespun Plaid #1	four half-square triangles,
Homespun Plaid #2	two 2 1/2" squares,
Homespun Plaid #3	two 2 1/2" squares, and
Light Homespun	four quarter-square triangles.

There will be some 2 1/2" squares left over. These are reserved for the cornerstones.

Select one of the thirty-five sets to piece a block. Use the 2 1/2" squares to piece a four patch unit. Press the seam allowances in the directions shown by the arrows.

make 1

Attach the quarter-square triangles of light homespun to the four patch. Sew the triangles onto two opposite sides first. Press the seam allowances toward the triangles. Add the remaining two triangles. Press the seam allowances toward the triangles. Trim the dog ears. For more detailed instruction on piecing a square within a square section see page 30 of the *Prints Charming* pattern.

make 1

Add the four half-square triangles to the unit from above to complete the block. First add the triangles to two opposite sides. Press the seam allowances toward the triangles. Complete the block. Press the seam allowances toward the triangles. Trim the dog ears. Repeat the above steps to make all thirty-five blocks.

one block
make 35

Completing the Quilt Top

Measure your blocks to determine their average size. They should measure 8 1/2" square and will finish to 8". From the sashing fabric, cut six strips that are the same width as your blocks (8 1/2" or your block's average size). Cut the 8 1/2" wide strips into eighty-two rectangles that are 2 1/2" x 8 1/2".

Sew together seven rows that consist of six sashes and five blocks which alternate. Press the seam allowances toward the sashes. Sew together eight rows that consist of six cornerstones (2 1/2" squares that were cut at the beginning of the pattern) and five sashes. Press the seam allowances toward the sashes. Refer to the photo on page 18 if necessary.

Sew the rows together. Press the seam allowances toward the sashing/cornerstone rows. Add borders with overlapped corners. Cut the borders 7 1/2" wide to finish the quilt shown in the photo. See page 10 for more information on borders.

Option to Consider

Queen Size

A queen size quilt will require seventy-two blocks (eight blocks per row/nine rows). The quilt will measure a generous 96" x 106". A full size or less generous queen size could be made with fifty-six blocks (seven blocks per row/eight rows).

With the same fabric placement as the twin version you will need the following for the seventy-two block quilt top:

Fabric	Amount
homespun fat quarters	18 fat quarters
light homespun	1 3/4 yards
sashing	2 3/4 yards
border	2 7/8 yards

Two Fabric Snail's Trail

The size of the quilt shown on page 17 is 42" x 54", a wall or small lap size. This variation was included to show how some of these patterns can be very effective with fewer fabrics. Other patterns that work well with fewer fabrics are *Delectable Mountains*, *Hot Apple Cider*, and *Rocky Mountain Puzzle*.

Fabric Requirements

Light Fabric	**1 1/2 yards**
Dark Fabric (includes binding)	**2 3/8 yards**
Backing	**2 3/4 yards**

Cutting

Light Fabric

Cut two strips 6 1/2" wide.
    Cut these strips into twelve 6 1/2" squares.

Cut two strips 4 1/4" wide.
    Cut these strips into twelve 4 1/4" squares.
        Cut these squares twice, diagonally, to make four quarter-square triangles from each square.   Yield: 48 triangles

Cut three strips 3 7/8" wide.
    Cut these strips into twenty-four 3 7/8" squares.
        Cut these squares once, diagonally, to make two half-square triangles from each square.   Yield: 48 triangles

Cut three strips 2" wide.

Dark Fabric

Cut five strips 6 1/2" wide.
    Cut these strips into twenty 6 1/2" squares and fourteen 3 1/2" x 6 1/2" rectangles.

Cut one strip 4 1/4" wide.
    Cut this strip into nine 4 1/4" squares.
        Cut these squares twice, diagonally, to make four quarter-square triangles from each square.   Yield: 36 triangles

Cut three strips 3 7/8" wide.
    Cut these strips into twenty-four 3 7/8" squares.
        Cut these squares once, diagonally, to make two half-square triangles from each square.   Yield: 48 triangles

Cut one strip 2 3/8" wide.
    Cut this strip into fourteen 2 3/8" squares.
        Cut these squares once, diagonally, to make two half-square triangles from each square.   Yield: 28 triangles

Cut three strips 2" wide.

Piecing

Sew the 2" wide strips of light and dark into pairs to make three panels like the one shown below. Press the seam allowances toward the dark strips.

Crosscut the panels into forty-eight sections that are 2" wide.

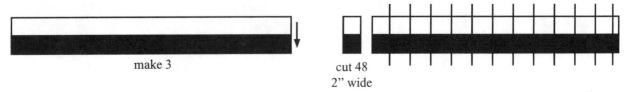

make 3

cut 48
2" wide

Set aside fourteen of the sections from above. Sew the remaining thirty-four into pairs to make seventeen four patch units. Press the seam allowances to one side.

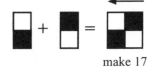

make 17

Sew a light quarter-square triangle to two opposite sides of the four patches. _**Be sure that all of the four patches are rotated into the position shown.**_ Press the seam allowances toward the triangles.

make 17

Sew a dark quarter-square triangle to the remaining two sides of the units from above. Press the seam allowances toward the dark triangles. Trim the dog ears. For more detailed instruction on piecing the square within a square section see page 30 of the _Prints Charming_ pattern.

make 17

Sew two light half-square triangles to each of the units from above. _**Again, be aware of their positions.**_ Press the seam allowances toward the half-square triangles.

make 17

Add two large dark half-square triangles to finish the blocks. Press the seam allowances toward the dark half-square triangles. Trim the dog ears.

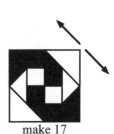

make 17

Making the Border Blocks

Sew two small dark half-square triangles to the fourteen reserved crosscut sections. _**It is very important that the triangles and crosscut section are all positioned exactly as shown.**_ Press the seam allowances in the directions shown by the arrows. Trim the dog ears.

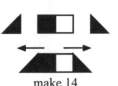

make 14

Add a quarter-square triangle of light fabric to the top of each unit. Press the seam allowances toward the light triangle. Trim the dog ears.

make 14

Add a light half-square triangle to each of the units. _**Make sure you are sewing it to the correct side.**_ Press the seam allowances toward the half-square triangle. Add a large dark half-square triangle to the units. Press the seam allowances toward the large dark triangles. Trim the dog ears.

make 14

Add a 3 1/2" x 6 1/2" rectangle of dark to each section to complete the border blocks. Press the seam allowances toward the rectangle.

make 14

Two Fabric *Snail's Trail* Layout
The quilt has been rotated sideways to conserve space.

Arrange the blocks and 6 1/2" squares to complete the pattern. Sew the blocks into horizontal rows. Press all seam allowances toward the plain 6 1/2" squares of both light and dark. Sew the rows together. Press the seam allowances to one side.

Option to Consider

Queen Size

The following is required for a queen size quilt top using the same layout as shown above:

fifty-six 6 1/2" squares of dark (seven per row/eight rows),
forty-two 6 1/2" squares of light (six per row/seven rows),
seventy-one snail's trail blocks, and
twenty-six border blocks.

In addition, you will need to add 6" wide borders to the quilt. Cut them 6 1/2" wide. The finished quilt will measure 90" x 102".

The queen size requires more yardage:

Light	4 1/2 yards
Dark	8 1/2 yards (The dark includes 3 1/2 yards of fabric for the borders and binding.)
Backing	8 1/4 yards

Snails in the Garden

The size of the quilt shown on page 19 is 62" x 86", a twin size. I used twenty-four fat quarters of both values for more variety. It was a less efficient use of fabric and resulted in more scraps, but I am happy with the results. Construction of this quilt will require experience with working on a design wall and basic knowledge of the Snail's Trail pattern.

Fabric Requirements

Twelve Light Fat Quarters	
Twelve Dark Fat Quarters	
Inner Border	**5/8 yard**
Outer Border	**2 1/4 yards**
Binding	**7/8 yard**
Backing	**5 1/4 yards**

Cutting

Fat Quarters

All of the fat quarters are cut in the same way. Stack the fat quarters as directed in the general directions. Make three stacks of eight fabrics.

Cut strips *perpendicular to* the selvages as shown in figure 1.

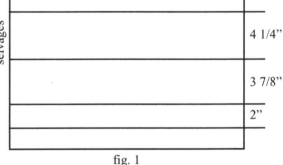

fig. 1

Cut one strip 6 1/2" wide from each fabric.
 From this strip cut a total of two 6 1/2" squares of each fabric.

Cut one strip 4 1/4" wide from each fabric.
 From this strip cut a total of two 4 1/4" squares of each fabric.
   Cut all of the 4 1/4" squares twice, diagonally, to make four quarter-square triangles from each square.
   Yield: 8 triangles of each fabric

Cut one strip 3 7/8" wide from each fabric.
 From this strip cut a total of four 3 7/8" squares of each fabric.
   Cut all of the 3 7/8" squares once, diagonally, to make two half-square triangles from each square.
   Yield: 8 triangles of each fabric

Cut one strip 2" wide from each fabric.
 From this strip cut a total of eight 2" squares of each fabric.

Piecing

Review the piecing instructions for the *Two Color Snail's Trail* on page 36 before beginning. This will familiarize you with the pattern. Use the photo on page 19 to layout your quilt on a design wall. I suggest that you only do a few rows at a time.

HINT: When using a design wall for a project like this one, begin by sitting at a table with a scrap (2" square, or so) of each fabric. Move the pieces around until you are happy with the placement of the fabrics relative to each other. Then, glue, tape, or staple these scraps in position onto a large piece of paper or poster board. This paste-up will become your key to a master plan and allow you to work on a few rows at a time.

make 48

Piece the snail's trail blocks, being sure that you get all the pieces where they belong to complete the spiral. Each block will have one half-square triangle, one quarter-square triangle, and one 2" square of four different fabrics in it.

Arrange the pieced blocks and 6 1/2" squares, alternately, as shown in the photo on page 19. Press all of the seam allowances toward the 6 1/2" squares. Sew the rows together. Press the seam allowances to one side.

Add borders with overlapped corners. Cut the inner border strips 2" wide. Inner border strips may be cut crossgrain, selvage to selvage. Cut the outer borders 6" wide to finish the quilt shown in the photo. See page 10 for more information on borders.

Options to Consider

Queen Size

A queen size quilt will require eighty-four snail's trail blocks and eighty-four 6 1/2" squares. The quilt will measure 87" x 99" when bordered in the same way as the twin size. For a more generous size (93" x 105") cut the outer borders 9" wide.

With the same fabric placement as the twin size version you will need the following for a queen size quilt top:

Fabric	Amount
light fat quarters	21 fat quarters
dark fat quarters	21 fat quarters
inner border	1 yard
outer border	2 3/4 yards

Scrappy

Another, more simple, option is to make a scrappier looking variation. Cut the same pieces. Place the fabrics randomly throughout the quilt. Just be sure to keep the lights and darks in the correct positions to create the overall pattern.

Rocky Mountain Puzzle

The size of the quilt shown on page 20 is 58 1/2" x 70", a lap size.

Fabric Requirements

Fifteen Dark Fat Quarters	
Light Tan	**1 3/4 yards**
Side and Corner Triangles	**1 3/8 yards**
Binding	**7/8 yard**
Backing	**3 3/4 yards**

Cutting

Fat Quarters

Stack the fat quarters as directed in the general directions. Make two stacks: seven fabrics in the first and eight fabrics in the second.

Cut off the selvages and cut strips *parallel to* the selvages as shown in figure 1.

Cut one strip 8 1/2" wide from each fabric.
 From this strip cut a total of two 8 1/2" squares of each fabric. The quilt requires twenty 8 1/2" squares, so do not worry about those fat quarters that are too small to yield two squares. You should have more than enough.

Cut one strip 3" wide from each fabric.
 From this strip cut a total of two 3" squares of each fabric.
  Trim the remainder of this strip to 2 1/2" and cut a total of four 2 1/2" squares of each fabric.

Cut two strips 2 7/8" wide from each fabric.
 From these two strips cut a total of ten 2 7/8" squares of each fabric.

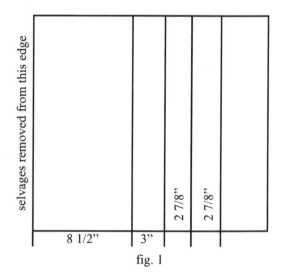

fig. 1

Light Tan

Cut eleven strips 2 7/8" wide.
 From these strips cut 150 squares (2 7/8").

Cut twelve strips 1 1/4" wide.
 From these strips cut sixty 1 1/4" x 4 1/2" rectangles and sixty 1 1/4" x 3" rectangles.

Side and Corner Triangles

Cut two strips 14" wide.
 From these strips cut five 14" squares.
  Cut the five 14" squares twice, diagonally, to make four quarter-square triangles from each square. Yield: 20 triangles

Cut one strip 8 1/8" wide.
 From this strip cut two 8 1/8" squares.
  Cut the two 8 1/8" squares once, diagonally, to make two half-square triangles from each square. Yield: 4 triangles

Piecing

Use one of the following two methods to make half-square triangle units from all of the 2 7/8" squares of light and fat quarter fabrics. Make 300 units, twenty of each fat quarter fabric.

make 20 of
each fabric

Method 1

Place a light square, right sides together, on top of each fat quarter fabric square. Cut the pairs of squares in half, diagonally, to make two pairs of half-square triangles. Chain piece the pairs of triangles on the diagonal to make half-square triangle units like the one shown above at the right. Press the seam allowances toward the fat quarter fabric. Trim the dog ears.

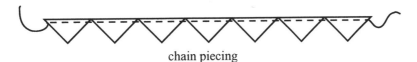

chain piecing

Method 2

You may prefer to draw a diagonal line from corner to corner on the pair of squares, stitch 1/4" away from this line along both sides of it, and then cut on the drawn line. Press the seam allowances toward the fat quarter fabric. Trim the dog ears.

Completing the Blocks

Sew a 1 1/4" x 3" rectangle to two opposite sides of all the 3" squares of fat quarter fabric. Press the seam allowances toward the rectangles.

make 30

Add the 1 1/4" x 4 1/2" rectangles to the units from directly above. Press the seam allowances toward the rectangles.

make 30

Assemble the blocks using only one fat quarter fabric in each block.

For each block sew two pairs of half-square triangles together as shown. Press the seam allowances in the direction shown by the arrow.

make 60 two
per block

41

Sew the pairs of half-square triangles to the square units. Press the seam allowances toward the square units.

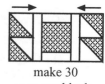

make 30
one per block

Sew the remaining half-square triangle units and the 2 1/2" squares into rows as shown directly at the right. Press the seam allowances in the directions shown by the arrows.

make 60
two per block

Complete all thirty blocks. Press the seam allowances toward the center row.

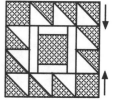

make 30 blocks

Completing the Quilt Top

Refer to the photo on page 20 while laying out the blocks. Arrange the blocks on point, placing five blocks in each of the six rows.

Put the 8 1/2" squares in place between the pieced blocks. Place the side triangles and corner triangles around the outer edges of the quilt.

Sew the blocks into diagonal rows. The side triangles and corner triangles are oversized to allow the other blocks to float away from the edges of the quilt. Align them as shown in the sample row below. Press the seam allowances away from the pieced blocks. Trim the large dog ears as shown below.

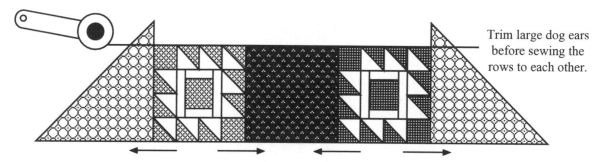

Trim large dog ears before sewing the rows to each other.

Sew the rows together. Press the seam allowances to one side.

Option to Consider

Queen Size

A queen size quilt will require forty-two blocks (six blocks per row/seven rows). With the addition of 10" wide borders the quilt will measure 88" x 99".

For this queen size quilt top you will need the following:

Fabric	Amount
dark fat quarters	21 fat quarters
light tan	2 1/4 yards
side & corner triangles	1 3/4 yards
added border	2 3/4 yards

Ninety-Six Miles an Hour

The size of the quilt shown on page 24 is 64" x 88", a twin size.

Fabric Requirements

Twelve light fat quarters*

Sixteen dark fat quarters*

*Consider purchasing two more lights and four more darks just to have on hand if you run short while piecing the border.

Inner Border	**5/8 yard**
Binding	**7/8 yard**
Backing	**5 1/4 yards**

Cutting

Light Fat Quarters

Stack *eight* of the twelve fat quarters as directed in the general directions. The remaining four will be cut differently.

Cut strips *perpendicular to* the selvages as shown in figure 1 on the following page.

Cut one strip 3 7/8" wide from each fabric.
From this strip cut a total of four 3 7/8" squares of each fabric. Label these A.

Cut one strip 3 1/2" wide from each fabric.
From this strip cut a total of four 3 1/2" squares of each fabric. Label these B.

Cut one strip 2 1/2" wide from each fabric.
From this strip cut a total of eight 2 1/2" squares of each fabric. Label these C.

Cut two strips 2" wide from each fabric.
From these two strips cut a total of
two 2" x 6 1/2" rectangles (Label these D.),
four 2" x 3 1/2" rectangles (Label these E.), and
four 2" squares (Label these F.) of each fabric.

Remaining Four Light Fat Quarters

Stack the remaining four fat quarters as directed in the general directions.

Cut strips *perpendicular to* the selvages as shown in figure 2 on the following page.

Cut one strip 3 7/8" wide from each fabric.
From this strip cut a total of four 3 7/8" squares of each fabric. These squares are more A pieces. Put them with the other A's.

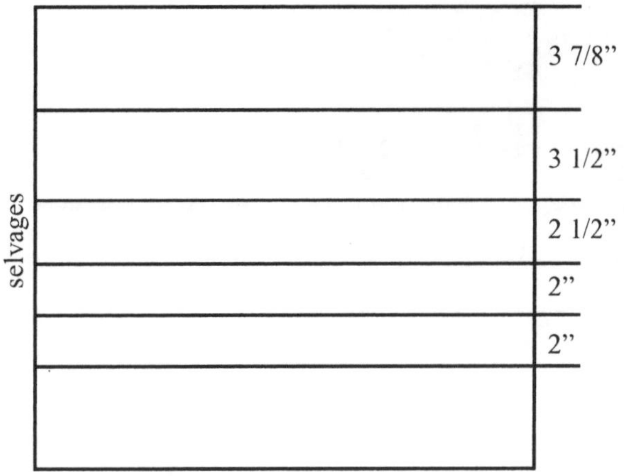

fig. 1

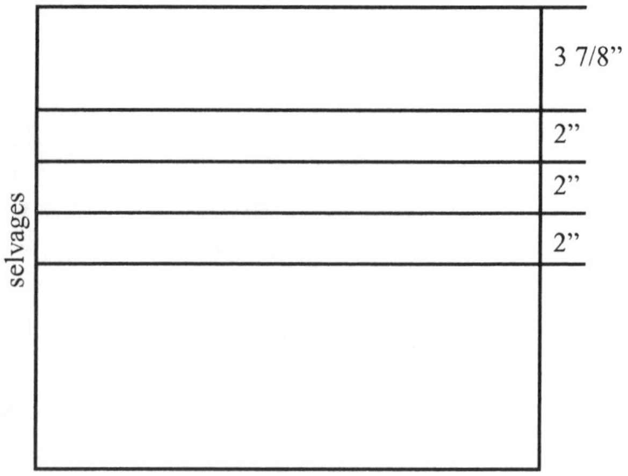

fig. 2

Remaining Four Light Fat Quarters, Continued

Cut three strips 2" wide from each fabric.
    From these three strips cut a total of
    eight 2" x 3 1/2" rectangles (Label these E.) and
    eight 2" squares (Label these F.) of each fabric. Put them with the other E's and F's.

When you have finished cutting the light fabrics you should have the following pieces.

A -- forty-eight 3 7/8" squares
B -- thirty-two 3 1/2" squares
C -- sixty-four 2 1/2" squares
D -- sixteen 2" x 6 1/2" rectangles
E -- sixty-four 2" x 3 1/2" rectangles
F -- sixty-four 2" squares

Dark Fat Quarters

Stack the fat quarters as directed in the general directions. Make two stacks of eight fabrics.

Cut strips ***perpendicular to*** the selvages as shown in figure 3 on the following page.

Cut one strip 3 7/8" wide from each fabric.
    From this strip cut a total of five 3 7/8" squares of each fabric. Label these G.

Cut one strip 3 1/2" wide from each fabric.
    From this strip cut a total of two 3 1/2" squares of each fabric. Label these H.

Cut one strip 2 1/2" wide from each fabric.
    From this strip cut a total of five 2 1/2" squares of each fabric. Label these I.

Cut two strips 2" wide from each fabric.
    From these two strips cut a total of
    three 2" x 6 1/2" rectangles (Label these J.),
    four 2" x 3 1/2" rectangles (Label these K.),
    and two 2" squares (Label these L.) of each fabric.

When you have finished cutting the dark fabrics you should have the following pieces.

G -- eighty 3 7/8" squares
H -- thirty-two 3 1/2" squares
I -- eighty 2 1/2" squares
J -- forty-eight 2" x 6 1/2" rectangles
K -- sixty-four 2" x 3 1/2" rectangles
L -- thirty-two 2" squares

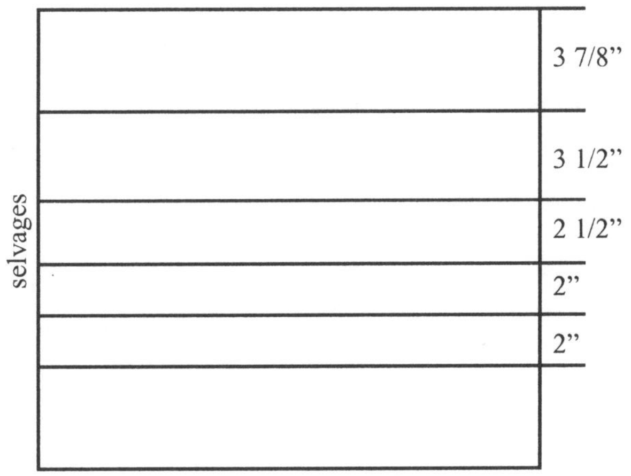

	3 7/8"
	3 1/2"
	2 1/2"
	2"
	2"

selvages

fig. 3

Save all remaining fabric, light and dark, to use when piecing your border.

Piecing

Rail Blocks

Use all of the D's and J's to piece sixteen rail blocks. Place a D at the top of each block, and place three J's below it in a pleasing order that is generally darker as it goes to the bottom of the block. Press the seam allowances in one direction, away from the D's.

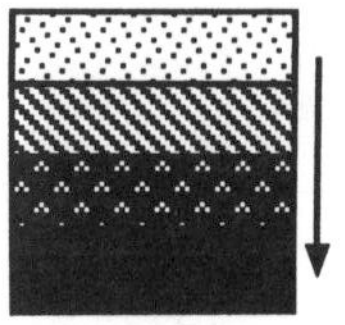

rail block
make 16

Nine Patch Blocks

Use all of the C's and I's to piece sixteen nine patch blocks. Make each block with only two fabrics, four squares of one light and five squares of one dark.

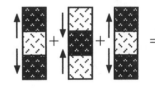

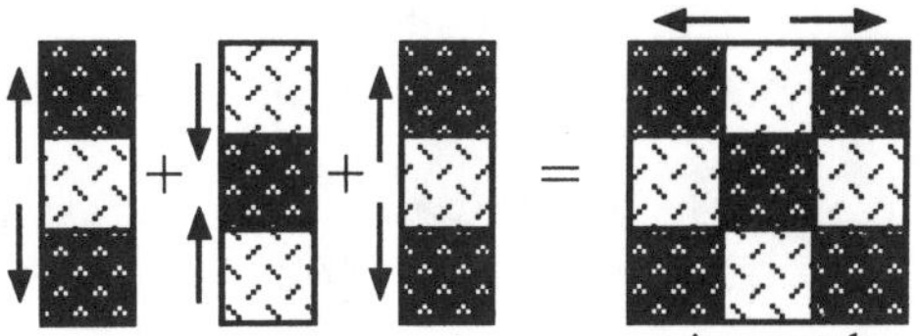

nine patch
make 16

Pinwheel Blocks

Use sixteen pairs of A's (thirty-two squares) and sixteen pairs of G's (thirty-two squares) to piece sixteen pinwheel blocks. Make each block with only two fabrics, two squares of one light and two squares of one dark.

make 4
per block

To make a pinwheel, place one square of A and one square of G, right sides together. Repeat with a second A and a second G. Use the same two fabrics as the first pair. Cut both pairs once, diagonally, into half-square triangles. Stitch the diagonal seam of each pair to make four half-square triangle units. Press the seam allowances toward the dark. Trim the dog ears. See page 41, if necessary, for more instruction and a second method for making half-square triangle units.

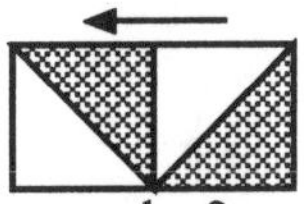

make 2
per block

Sew the half-square units into two pairs. Press the seam allowances in the direction shown by the arrow. Sew these pairs together to complete a pinwheel block. Press the seam allowances to one side.

Repeat to make sixteen pinwheels.

pinwheel
make 16

Broken Dishes Blocks

Use the remaining A's and G's to piece sixteen broken dishes blocks. Make each block with three fabrics, one square of light, two squares of one dark, and one square of a second dark.

To make a block, place the two squares of G that are the same fabric onto the other two fabrics, right sides together. Make half-square triangle units from these as you did for the pinwheel blocks. Press the seam allowances toward the darker fabrics. Trim the dog ears.

Arrange the units in one of the two ways shown directly at the right. The blocks in the quilt shown on page 24 are made like the one on the left. It may be necessary to press the seam allowances of some units in the opposite direction so that they will nest together for matching the seam lines. Otherwise, pin to match the seams.

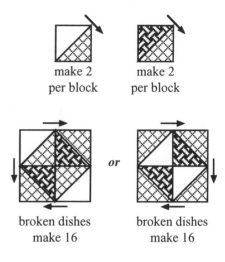

make 2 per block   make 2 per block

broken dishes make 16   *or*   broken dishes make 16

Bow Tie Blocks

Use all of the B's, H's, and L's to piece sixteen bow tie blocks. Each block uses only two fabrics, one light and one dark.

Use the B's, the L's, and a sew and flip technique, to make thirty-two units like the one shown in figure 4. Stitch along the diagonal as shown by the dashed line. Check your work. If it is correct, trim the excess, leaving 1/4" for seam allowances. Press the seam allowances toward the dark.

Complete the bow tie blocks. Press the seam allowances in the directions shown by the arrows.

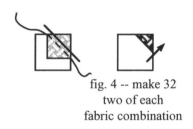

fig. 4 -- make 32 two of each fabric combination

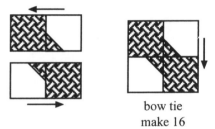

bow tie make 16

Twinkle Toes Star Blocks

Use all of the E's, F's, and K's to piece sixteen stars. Each block uses only two fabrics, one light and one dark.

To piece a star use four E's and four F's of the same light fabric and four K's of one dark fabric.

Place a 2" square of the light fabric, right sides together, onto one end of each rectangle of dark. Use the sew and flip technique as described above in the bow tie block, to make four units like the one shown in figure 5. Make sure all units look exactly like the one shown. *Make no reverses!* Check your work. Trim the excess. Press the seam allowances toward the dark.

Sew the units from above to the F's. Press the seam allowances toward F.

Complete the star block. Press the seam allowances in the directions shown by the arrows. Repeat to make sixteen stars.

fig. 5 make 4 per star

make 4 per star

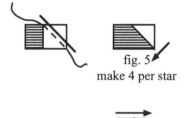

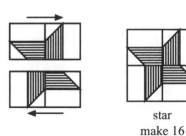

star make 16

Completing the Quilt Top

Refer to the photo on page 24 while completing the quilt. Arrange the ninety-six blocks randomly into twelve rows of eight blocks. Sew the blocks into horizontal rows. Press the seam allowances of the odd rows to the left. Press the seam allowances of the even rows to the right. Sew the rows together. Press the seam allowances to one side.

Cut strips from all of the remaining fabrics. Cut these strips perpendicular to the selvage. Vary the widths from 1 1/4" to 3". Use them randomly to strip-piece seven or eight panels that measure approximately 15". It is impossible to give an exact number of panels and sections due to the random widths of the pieces. Press the seam allowances to one side. Crosscut these panels into 6 3/4" wide sections.

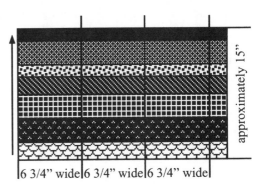

approximately 15"

6 3/4" wide | 6 3/4" wide | 6 3/4" wide

panels for borders
make 7 or 8

Determine the length of your quilt. Sew enough of the 6 3/4" wide sections together, end on end to make two borders for the sides of the quilt. Trim the borders to shorten them or use scraps to add to the length of the borders in order to make them fit.

Cut eight strips, selvage to selvage, 2" wide from the inner border fabric. Use four of these strips, two per side, to piece two borders to fit the strip-pieced side borders of your quilt. Attach an inner border to each strip-pieced border. Press the seam allowances toward the inner border.

Sew the side borders to the quilt. Press the seam allowances toward the borders.

Determine the width of your quilt. Sew strip-pieced sections together to make two borders to fit the width of the quilt.

Use the remaining four 2" wide strips of inner border fabric to piece inner borders to fit the top and bottom strip-pieced borders. Attach the inner borders to the top and bottom borders. Press the seam allowances toward the inner borders. Add the borders to the quilt. Press the seam allowances toward the borders.

Options to Consider

Queen Size

A queen size quilt will require 168 blocks (twelve blocks per row/fourteen rows). The finished quilt will measure 88" x 100" if the same borders are added. To construct the 168 blocks you may choose to make twenty-eight of each of the six patterns. These blocks finish to 6". I suggest that you add other simple 6" blocks to the quilt for more interest instead of making so many of only six different blocks. You will certainly be able to find more patterns in your books and magazines.

With the same blocks and fabric placement as the twin version you will need the following for the queen size quilt top:

Fabric	Amount
light fat quarters	24 fat quarters
dark fat quarters	32 fat quarters
inner border	1 yard

Three Crib Size Quilts

A small crib size quilt can be made with thirty blocks (five blocks per row/six rows). With ninety-six blocks, there are enough blocks to make three crib quilts and have six blocks left to enlarge one of the quilts, to use on the back, or to use in another project.

When assembling the crib quilts, you may choose to make three sampler quilts or three quilts which use two blocks each in an alternating setting. See below for some suggested layouts.

Consider adding sashing or other setting pieces to these suggested layouts for even more variation.

Layouts for Crib Size Quilts

The quilts shown below measure 30" x 36" without borders. Add borders as desired.

Samplers

Two Alternating Blocks

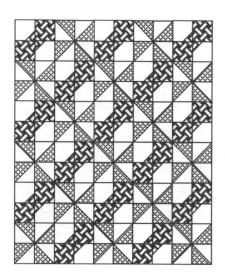  

Delectable Mountains

The size of the quilt shown on page 27 is 67" x 89 1/2", a twin size.

Fabric Requirements

Nine light fat quarters*
>*If you prefer to use one background fabric, purchase 2 1/4 yards of that fabric and use it to cut thirty-six 8 3/8" squares of light.

Fourteen dark fat quarters

Border	**2 1/2 yards**
Binding	**1 yard**
Backing	**5 1/2 yards**

Cutting

Fat Quarters

Cut each of the fat quarters into four 8 3/8" squares.
>Yield: 36 squares of light and 56 squares of dark

Border Fabric

Remove the selvages from the border fabric.

Cut (do not tear) two 8 3/8" panels along the length, as shown in figure 1.
>Cut nineteen 8 3/8" squares from these two panels.
>Yield: 19 squares

Cut or tear the remaining border fabric into four equal panels. There should be enough fabric to cut these between 3 1/2" and 4" wide. Reserve these to add borders to the quilt top.

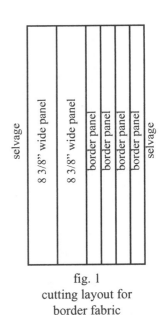

fig. 1
cutting layout for
border fabric

Piecing

If you are using different light fabrics like the quilt on page 27, you will need to work on a design wall.

First, cut all of the 8 3/8" squares once, diagonally, to make two half-square triangles from each (figure 2). Do not sew the triangles together yet. Begin arranging these on your design wall as shown on the next page. The solid black triangles are those that were cut from the border fabric.

fig. 2
cut all 111
squares into
half-square
triangles

row 1

row 2

fig. 3

Repeat the pattern of row 2, five "mountains" (dark fat quarters triangles), a border fabric triangle on each end, and four pairs of light or background triangles, to lay out rows 3 through 10. Repeat the pattern of row 1 to lay out row 11, the bottom row.

Sew the diagonal seam of each pair of triangles to complete the half-square triangle units. Press the seam allowances toward the "mountain" fabrics (the dark fat quarter fabrics). Trim the dog ears and measure the blocks. They should measure 8" square. Do just a few at a time, placing them back into position on the design wall.

It is very important that you follow these instructions carefully and exactly in order to get the diagonal seams slanting in the correct directions while having the fabrics in the desired positions! Work with one pair of blocks at a time from this point on.

Select the first two blocks of row 1. Rotate them so that they look exactly like those in figure 4.

Being careful not to change their positions, slice the two blocks vertically into 2" wide sections (figure 5). Figures 5 and 6 are enlarged to show detail.

The sections are labeled in figure 5 so you can see how to position them (figure 6) to make the mountain block.

Rearrange the sections as shown in figure 6. Sew them together to complete the mountain. Press all the seam allowances to the left.

Select the third and fourth blocks of row 1 and repeat the above instructions, being very careful that the blocks are rotated into the correct positions before slicing them (figure 7).

Continue across row 1 until you have pieced all five mountain blocks. Sew the blocks together and press the seam allowances toward the left.

All the seam allowances of the odd rows should be pressed to the left. All the seam allowances of the even rows should be pressed to the right. This way they will oppose one another and make matching the seam lines simple to do when sewing the rows together.

All of the remaining rows are constructed just like row 1, but they may look more confusing because of the placements of the fabrics when the blocks are rotated into position for slicing. See figures 8 through 13 on the next page to get you started.

first   second
block   block
row 1   row 1

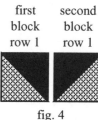

fig. 4

2" 2" 2" 2"   2" 2" 2" 2"

A   B   C   D   E   F   G   H

fig. 5

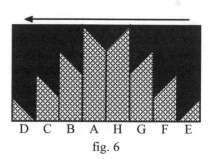

D   C   B   A   H   G   F   E

fig. 6

third   fourth
block   block
row 1   row 1

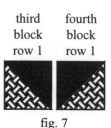

fig. 7

50

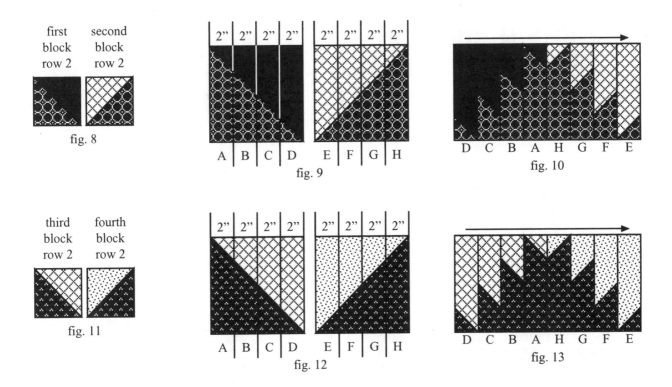

first block row 2   second block row 2

fig. 8

2" 2" 2" 2"   2" 2" 2" 2"

A B C D   E F G H

fig. 9

D C B A H G F E

fig. 10

third block row 2   fourth block row 2

fig. 11

2" 2" 2" 2"   2" 2" 2" 2"

A B C D   E F G H

fig. 12

D C B A H G F E

fig. 13

After constructing all eleven rows, sew them together. Press the seam allowances to one side.

Add borders to the quilt. See page 10 for more instruction on borders.

Options to Consider

Queen Size

A queen size quilt will require ninety-one blocks (seven blocks per row/thirteen rows). A sketch of the layout is shown on page 53. It is shown with only one background fabric.

With the same fabric placement as the twin size version you will need the following to complete the queen size quilt top:

Fabric	Amount	# of 8 3/8" Squares
light fat quarters	17 fat quarters, or 4 1/4 yards of one background fabric	66
dark fat quarters	23 fat quarters	91
border	3 1/2 yards	25**

**Cut the squares and borders as directed for the twin size. Your panels will be longer to allow for the additional squares and longer borders.

Borders for Another Quilt

The Delectable Mountain block finishes to 12" wide. Thus, it is a perfect pieced border for quilts made from 12" blocks. It may be used for quilts made with other sizes of blocks as long as an inner border has been added to bring the quilt up to a size that the Delectable Mountain borders will fit. Use one or two rows of mountains for the borders.

Stagger the Rows, Flip the Rows, or Do Both

Whether you are making a Delectable Mountains quilt or using the pattern for a border, consider staggering the rows, flipping the rows, or doing a combination of both. See the sketches on the following page for some ideas to get you started.

The second row is staggered a half block.

The second row is flipped vertically.

The second row is staggered a half block and flipped vertically.

Once you have decided how you want to position your blocks, be sure to press the seams so that they nest together when you sew the rows together. In other words, press the seam allowances of the odd rows to the left and press the seam allowances of the even rows to the right.

Scrappy Variation

Place the fabrics randomly for a scrappy variation. All that is necessary is to keep the "A" pieces where they belong, the "B" pieces where they belong, etc. This border is very effective when used on multiple fabric quilts. The light pieces can be multiple fabrics or a control fabric.

random placement of fabrics

Queen Size Layout

This quilt requires ninety-one blocks.

Stacked Bricks

The size of the quilt shown on page 26 is 86" x 103", a queen size.

Fabric Requirements

Sixteen light fat quarters	
Fourteen dark fat quarters	
Sashing	**2 3/4 yards**
Border	**2 3/4 yards**
Binding	**1 yard**
Backing	**8 yards**

Cutting

Light Fat Quarters

Stack the fat quarters as directed in the general directions. Make two stacks of eight fabrics.

Cut strips *perpendicular to* the selvages as shown in figure 1.

Cut five strips 3" wide from each fabric.

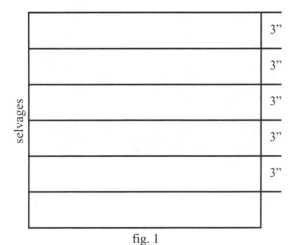

fig. 1

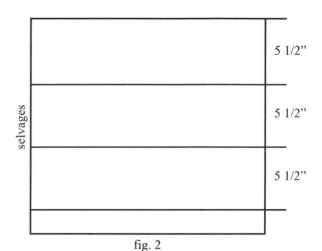

fig. 2

54

Dark Fat Quarters

Stack the fat quarters as directed in the general directions. Make two stacks of seven fabrics.

Cut strips *perpendicular to* the selvages as shown in figure 2 on the previous page.

Cut three strips 5 1/2" wide from each fabric.

Piecing

Sew a 3" strip of light fabric to both long edges of forty 5 1/2" strips of dark. Use the fabrics randomly so that each strip-pieced panel is different and has three different fabrics in it. Press the seam allowances toward the light strips. See figure 3. There will be two dark strips left over and not used in the quilt.

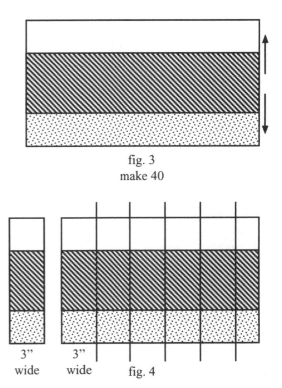

fig. 3
make 40

Crosscut each panel into six sections 3" wide (figure 4). The quilt requires a total of 240 sections.

Make five rows according to the following instructions. Each row will use 24 sections. Chain piece and make all five rows at the same time.

3" wide   3" wide   fig. 4

Position the second brick section so that the top of this second section is 1/4" above the top seam line of the first section. Because you pressed the seam allowances toward the light strip, the raw edges of the seam allowances of the first section and the top of the second section should be even. See the sketch at the right. Stitch five pairs, one pair for each row, as shown in figure 5. Do not press until the rows have been completed.

fig. 5

Continue adding sections, staggering as before, until you have five rows of 24 sections (figure 6). Press all of the seam allowances in one direction.

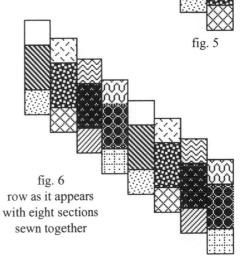

fig. 6
row as it appears
with eight sections
sewn together

fig. 7

Now make five rows that are the reverse of the first five. To do this, begin by staggering the second section so that the top seam line is 1/4" below the top edge of the first section. See figure 7. Again, chain piece and make all five rows at the same time.

55

Continue adding sections until you have five reverse rows of 24 sections (figure 8). Press all of the seam allowances in one direction.

Now it is time to square the ends of the rows. Working with one of the first five rows, locate the bottom finished corner of any one of the bricks. Cut across the row 1/4" below this point. See figure 9.

fig. 8
reverse row as it appears with eight sections sewn together

Sew the trimmed section to the top of that same row. Trim the top of the row 1/4" beyond the top finished corner of the first complete brick. Trim and complete the other four rows in the same manner.

Now, trim and complete the five reverse rows. See figure 10.

Trim the points of light fabrics along both sides of all rows. Do this by *aligning the 1/4" line of your ruler with the finished corners of the bricks* and trimming with your rotary cutter. By placing the 1/4" line on the finished corners, you have added a perfect 1/4" seam allowance to the rows while trimming.

Measure all of the trimmed rows. Be careful not to stretch them too much when measuring. It is best done on a flannel wall or carpeted floor. Holding the rows in the air or laying them on a slippery surface like a table will not give you an accurate measurement. Determine the average measurement.

Cut thirteen 2" wide strips along the *length* of your sashing fabric. This direction is parallel to the selvages and in the *opposite* direction from most strip cutting. Trim eleven of these to fit the length of your rows.

Alternate the rows so that every other row is a reverse row. Refer to the photo on page 26. Sew the rows and sashes together, matching the ends and centers, and pinning as necessary. Press the seam allowances toward the sashes.

fig. 9
Pick any spot that is 1/4" below the bottom corner of a finished brick and cut across the row.

cut
here

Sew the section that was at the bottom to the top of the same row, staggering it to fit.

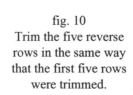

cut
here

fig. 10
Trim the five reverse rows in the same way that the first five rows were trimmed.

56

Measure the width of your quilt. Trim the last two sashes to this size. Attach one to the top and the second to the bottom of the quilt. Press the seam allowances toward the sashing.

Add borders with overlapped corners. Cut these borders 9" to 10" wide. See page 10 for more instruction on borders.

Options to Consider

As a Border

The stacked bricks pattern makes a great pieced border. However, it will take an experienced quilter to make it fit.

TIP: Make your pieced borders a bit larger than necessary to fit the quilt. Then, add a filler strip (an inner border) to float the pieced border away from the quilt and make it fit.

Smaller Bricks

This pattern is simple and fun in any size. To make a smaller quilt cut the strips of brick fabrics 4 1/2" wide and the strips of background fabrics 2 1/2" wide. Crosscut the panels 2 1/2" wide and continue, as directed.

Smaller still? Cut the strips of brick fabrics 3 1/2" wide and the strips of background fabrics 2" wide. Crosscut the panels 2" wide and continue.

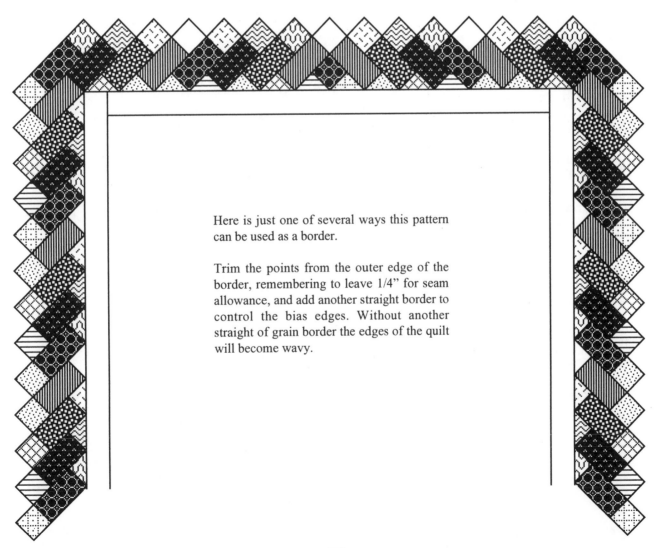

Here is just one of several ways this pattern can be used as a border.

Trim the points from the outer edge of the border, remembering to leave 1/4" for seam allowance, and add another straight border to control the bias edges. Without another straight of grain border the edges of the quilt will become wavy.

Hot Apple Cider

The size of the quilt shown on page 21 is 77 1/2" x 90 1/4", a full size.

Fabric Requirements

Fifteen golden tan fat quarters

Ten red fat quarters

Eight dark green fat quarters

Sashing	1 1/4 yards
Border	2 3/8 yards
Binding	1 yard
Backing	5 1/2 yards

Cutting

Golden Tan Fat Quarters

Stack the fat quarters as directed in the general directions. Make one stack of seven fabrics and one stack of eight fabrics.

Cut off the selvages and cut strips *parallel to* the selvages as shown in figure 1.

Cut one strip 7 1/4" wide from each fabric.
    From this strip cut a total of two 7 1/4" squares of each fabric.
        Cut the two 7 1/4" squares twice, diagonally, to make four quarter-square triangles from each square.   Yield: 8 triangles of each fabric

Cut one strip 4 1/4" wide from each fabric.
    From this strip cut a total of two 4 1/4" squares of each fabric.
        Cut the two 4 1/4" squares twice, diagonally, to make four quarter-square triangles from each square.
        Yield: 8 triangles of each fabric

Cut two strips 2" wide from each fabric.
    From these two strips cut a total of sixteen 2" squares of each fabric.

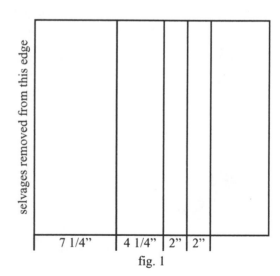

selvages removed from this edge

7 1/4"   4 1/4" 2" 2"

fig. 1

Red Fat Quarters

Stack the fat quarters as directed in the general directions. Make two stacks of five fabrics.

Cut strips *perpendicular to* the selvages as shown in figure 2.

Cut two strips 4 1/4" wide from each fabric.
    From these two strips cut a total of six 4 1/4" squares of each fabric, four from the first strip and two from the second. Reserve the remainder of the second strip for cutting the 3 1/2" pieces as directed below.
        Cut the six 4 1/4" squares twice, diagonally, to make four quarter-square triangles from each square.   Yield: 24 triangles of each fabric

Trim the remainder of the second 4 1/4" wide strip to 3 1/2". See photo 7 on page 9.
    From this piece cut a total of three 3 1/2" squares of each fabric.

Cut four strips 2" wide from each fabric.
    Use these strips to cut the trapezoids as directed below.

Cutting the Trapezoids

Follow these instructions exactly. Half of the trapezoids in this pattern are reverses of the others. The best way to cut them is to place one stack of 2" strips (the strips that you cut above) **wrong side up** on your cutting mat. Place a second stack of 2" wide strips of the same fabrics neatly aligned on top of the first. This second stack should be facing **right side up** (photo 10).

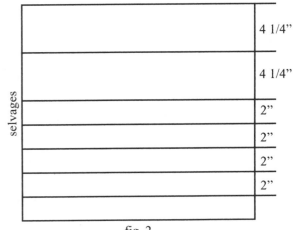

fig. 2

Cut trapezoids through all ten layers. Use the template on the next page or use the Omnigrid 96 or 96L triangle tool. See photos 11 (below) and 12 (following page) if you are using the Omnigrid 96 or 96L. Align the 3" mark with the long edge of the strip.

If you are using the template, you may want to tape it to the underside of any 45 degree triangle to make your own custom rotary cutting tool (photo 13 on the following page).

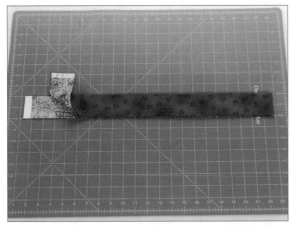

photo 10

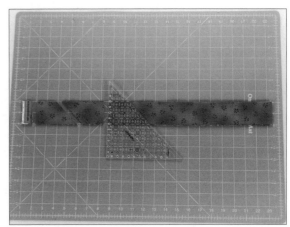

photo 11

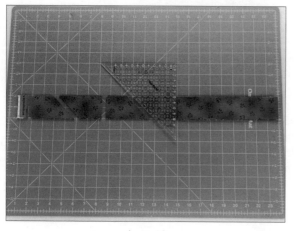

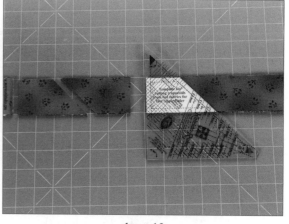

photo 12   photo 13

Align the remaining stacks of 2" wide strips as directed before, wrong sides together. Continue cutting trapezoids until you have cut twelve pairs of each fabric as shown (figure 3).

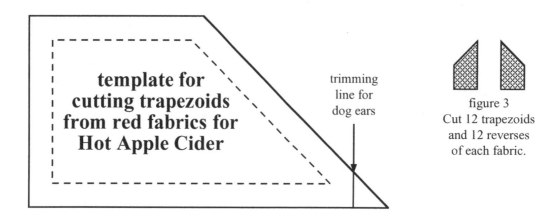

template for
cutting trapezoids
from red fabrics for
Hot Apple Cider

trimming
line for
dog ears

figure 3
Cut 12 trapezoids
and 12 reverses
of each fabric.

Dark Green Fat Quarters

Stack the fat quarters as directed in the general directions. Make one stack of eight fabrics.

Cut strips *perpendicular to* the selvages as shown in figure 4.

Cut five strips 2" wide from each fabric.
    From these strips cut forty-eight 2" squares of each fabric.

For the cornerstones of the quilt you will need forty-two squares that are cut 1 1/4". These may be cut from the remainder of one of your dark green fabrics, or you may cut five or six squares from each of the fabrics. I elected to use just one fabric.

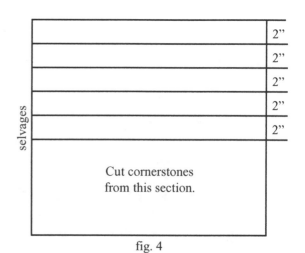

selvages

2"

2"

2"

2"

2"

Cut cornerstones
from this section.

fig. 4

Sashing and Borders

These should be cut when you are ready to sew them to the quilt.

Piecing

Organize your pieces into thirty sets prior to sewing. Each set will make one block. Use four fabrics for each block (one golden tan, two different reds, and one dark green). The pieces needed for one block are the following:

Golden tan	four large quarter-square triangles, four small quarter-square triangles, and eight 2" squares,
Red #1	eight quarter-square triangles and one 3 1/2" square,
Red #2	four trapezoids and four reverse trapezoids, and
Dark green	twelve 2" squares.

Select one set of the thirty to piece a block.

Use eight 2" squares of golden tan and eight 2" squares of dark green to piece four four patch units. Press the seam allowances in the directions shown by the arrows.

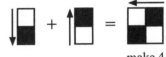

make 4

You may prefer to trim the dog ears of the trapezoids before sewing. See the template on the previous page for the trimming line. Sew a red #2 trapezoid to each of the four patches. _**Make sure the four patch is positioned exactly as shown and the finished unit looks like the one at the right.**_ Press the seam allowances toward the four patches.

make 4

Sew the remaining 2" squares of dark green to the ends of the reverse trapezoids. Press the seam allowances toward the squares.

make 4

Sew the units from above together to make four sections like the one shown directly at the right. Press the seam allowances toward the four patch. Trim the dog ears if you have not done so already.

make 4

Attach a quarter-square triangle of red #1 to each unit from above. For proper alignment, match the center of the triangle with the seam line. Press the seam allowances toward the triangle. Trim the dog ears.

make 4

Add a second quarter-square triangle of red #1 to the units you just completed. Center the triangle with the seam line. Press the seam allowances toward this triangle. Trim the dog ears.

make 4

Attach the smaller quarter-square triangles of golden tan to the sides of the 3 1/2" square of red #1. Sew the triangles onto two opposite sides first. Press the seam allowances toward the triangles. Add the remaining two triangles. Press the seam allowances toward the triangles. Trim the dog ears. For more detailed instruction on piecing the square within a square section see page 30 of the *Prints Charming* pattern.

make 1

Arrange the five pieced units and four large quarter-square triangles of golden tan to make the block. Sew the pieces together making diagonal rows. Press the seam allowances as shown by the arrows. Sew the rows together. Press the seam allowances away from the center row. Trim the dog ears.

Repeat the above steps with the remaining twenty-nine sets of pieces to make thirty blocks.

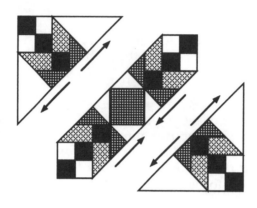

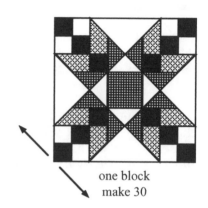

one block
make 30

Completing the Quilt Top

Measure your blocks to determine their average size. They should measure 12 1/2" square, and will finish to 12".

From the sashing fabric, cut three strips that are that are 12 1/2" wide (or as wide as the average size of your blocks). Cut the 12 1/2" wide strips into seventy-one rectangles that are 1 1/4" x 12 1/2".

Sew together six rows that consist of six sashes and five blocks which alternate. Press the seam allowances toward the sashes.

Sew together seven rows that consist of six cornerstones (cut at the beginning of the pattern) and five sashes. Press the seam allowances toward the sashes.

Sew the rows together. Refer to the photo on page 21 if necessary. Press the seam allowances toward the sashing/cornerstone rows.

Add borders with overlapped corners. Cut the borders 7" wide to finish the quilt shown in the photo. See page 10 for more instruction on borders.

Options to Consider

Queen Size

A queen size quilt will require forty-two blocks (six blocks per row/seven rows). The quilt will measure 90 1/4" x 103".

With the same fabric placement as the full size version you will need the following to complete the queen size quilt top:

Fabric	Amount
golden tan fat quarters	21 fat quarters
red fat quarters	14 fat quarters
dark green	11 fat quarters
border	2 3/4 yards

On Point Setting

For a completely different look set these blocks on point. Use sashing or alternating plain blocks. See the following page for an example.

Wider Sashes and Cornerstones

If you use a common background fabric instead of the golden tan fat quarters, cut the sashes from this background fabric. Cut them 2" wide. Cut the dark green cornerstones 2" square. The blocks will "disappear" leaving behind a secondary pattern. See the following page for an on point version of this setting.

Fewer Fabrics

This pattern can be made from yardage of four fabrics, as you can see by the illustration on the following page.

Optional Setting for *Hot Apple Cider*

This quilt uses eighteen blocks. The sashes are cut 2" x 12 1/2" and the cornerstones are cut 2" square. The side triangles are quarter-square triangles that are cut from three 20 3/8"squares. The corner triangles are half-square triangles that are cut from two 11 1/2" squares. Before the addition of any borders, the quilt measures 62 1/4" x 82". With the addition of borders it could fit a twin (Cut the borders 5" wide.) or full (Cut the borders 10" wide.) size bed.

Confined to Quarters

The size of the quilt shown on page 22 is 63" x 72", a lap size.

Fabric Requirements

Fifteen light fat quarters

Fifteen dark fat quarters

Binding   **3/4 yard**

Backing   **4 yards**

Cutting

Fat Quarters

All of the fat quarters are cut in exactly the same way. Stack the fat quarters as directed in the general directions. Make four or five stacks with six to eight fat quarters in each stack.

Cut off the selvages and cut strips *parallel to* the selvages as shown in figure 1.

Cut one strip 3 7/8" wide from each fabric.
   Cut this strip into a total of four 3 7/8" squares of each fabric.
      Cut these squares once, diagonally, to make two half-square triangles from each square.   Yield: 8 triangles of each fabric

Cut three strips 3 1/2" wide from each fabric.
   Cut these three strips into a total of two 3 1/2" squares and sixteen 2" x 3 1/2" rectangles of each fabric.

Cut one strip 2 3/4" wide from each fabric.

Cut one strip 2" wide from each fabric.

Piecing

fig. 1

Organize your fabrics before you begin to sew.

Pair each of the dark fabrics with a light fabric to make fifteen sets of two fabrics, one light and one dark per set. Use your fabrics in pairs throughout the construction of the quilt. One pair of fabrics will make four blocks. Two of the blocks will have light backgrounds and two of the blocks will have dark backgrounds.

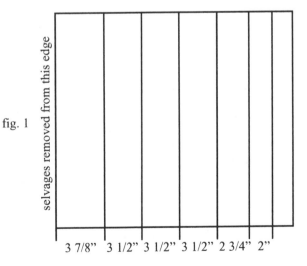

Use all the pieces from one pair of fabrics to make the first four blocks.

Sew the 2 3/4" strip of dark to the to the 2" strip of light and sew the 2 3/4" strip of light to the 2" strip of dark to make the panels shown directly at the right.

Press the seam allowances toward the 2 3/4" wide strips.

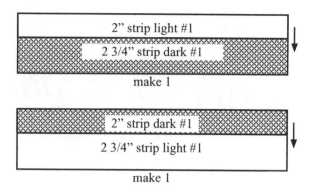

2" strip light #1
2 3/4" strip dark #1
make 1

2" strip dark #1
2 3/4" strip light #1
make 1

Crosscut each of the panels from above into eight sections that are 2" wide. See below.

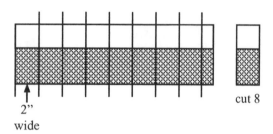

cut 8

2"
wide

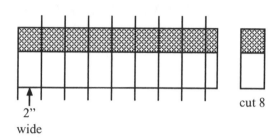

cut 8

2"
wide

Sew the units from above into four patches as shown. Use two sections that are from the same panel for each four patch. *These will not match at the seam line.* Just match the ends and sew. Make four of each combination.

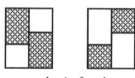

make 4 of each
combination

Clip the seam allowances at the center of each four patch and press as shown. For best results, clip all the way through the stitching. You will soon slice the units through this point.

These four patch units should measure 3 1/2" x 4 1/4" at this time.

Cut these units into "scraps" triangles. See the following page for more instruction. This technique and variations of it are the bases for all of the quilts in my book *Scraps to You, Too.*

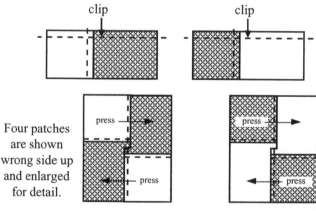

clip   clip

Four patches
are shown
wrong side up
and enlarged
for detail.

press

press

press

press

Sew the "scraps" triangles to the half-square triangles that were cut at the beginning to make Bird in the Air blocks as shown at the right. Pay attention to which pieces use the light triangles and which use the dark triangles. Press the seam allowances toward the large half-square triangles. Trim the dog ears.

make 8 of each
Bird in the Air blocks

Sew the sixteen 2" x 3 1/2" rectangles of light to the sixteen 2" x 3 1/2" rectangles of dark. Press the seam allowances of eight units toward the light and press the seam allowances of the remaining eight units toward the dark.

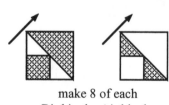

make 16

Read through this page before cutting. ***Do not cut the pieces exactly from corner to corner!*** Use an Omnigrid 96 or 96L triangle tool or make a template from the actual size drawing below. For a template, trace the triangular area in the upper right which is outlined by the bold line.

The Omnigrid 96 triangle is a tool, not a ruler. What that means is that the seam allowances are built into it. The finished size of the units is 3". Align the 3" line with the edge of the four patch as shown in the sketch below. Lay your tool on the actual size drawing to see how it works.

Ready, Set, Cut!

Read the checklist of tips at the lower right. Okay, cut! You now have what I affectionately refer to as "scraps" triangles.

If you reversed the pieces when sewing your four patches, don't despair. Just rotate the four patch a quarter turn and align the unit on the 3" line as shown at the right (or reverse the template).

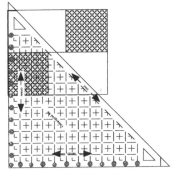

TIPS:

Before making the cut, align the seam lines of the four patch unit so they are square with the grid lines on the tool or template.

Check at the center of the unit to be sure that both pieces you make from the four patch will have a 1/4" seam allowance along the diagonal.

Be sure that you are cutting through the rectangle pieces that meet in the center of the unit and not the squares that are in the two opposite corners.

Don't be alarmed by the blunt corner on one tip of each "scraps" triangle. The missing part is just a dog ear.

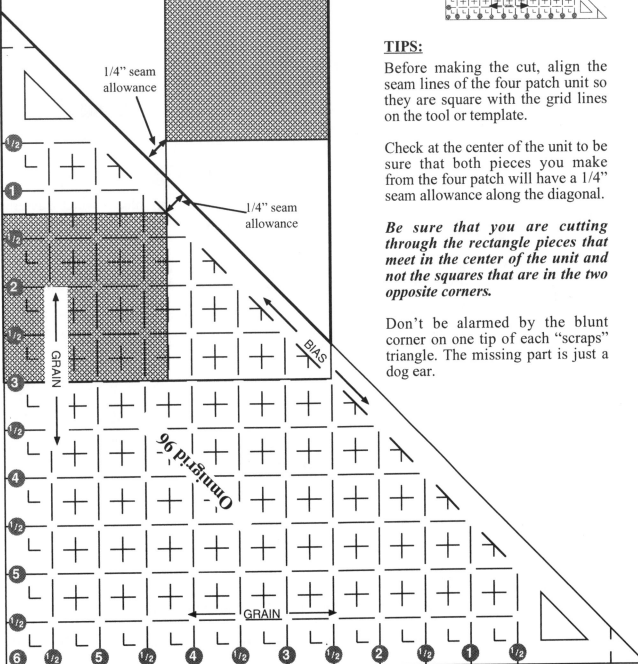

1/4" seam allowance

1/4" seam allowance

BIAS

Omnigrid 96

GRAIN

GRAIN

Sew eight  sections to the Bird in the Air blocks to make the rows shown at the right. As always, press the seams in the directions shown by the arrows.

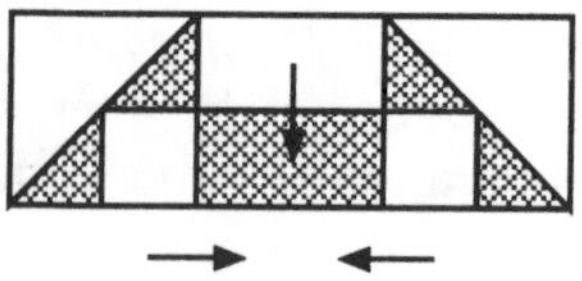

make 4 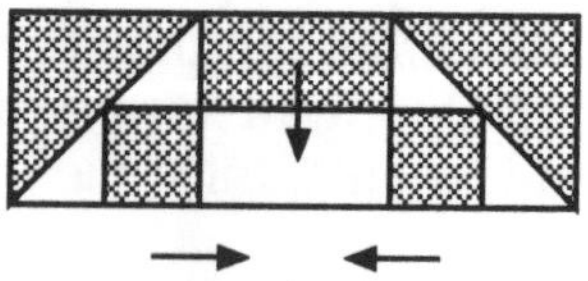   make 4

Sew the remaining eight  sections to the 3 1/2" squares of both fabrics. Press as shown by the arrows.

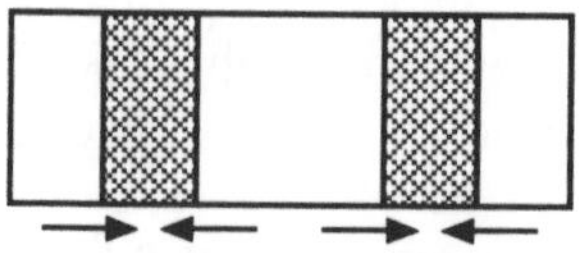

make 2 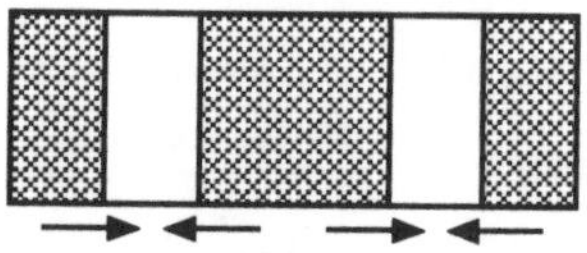   make 2

Sew together the sections from above to complete the blocks. Press the seam allowances toward the middle row.

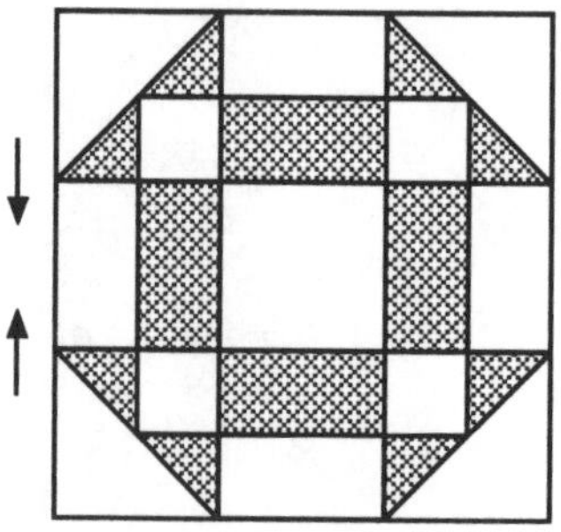

make 2 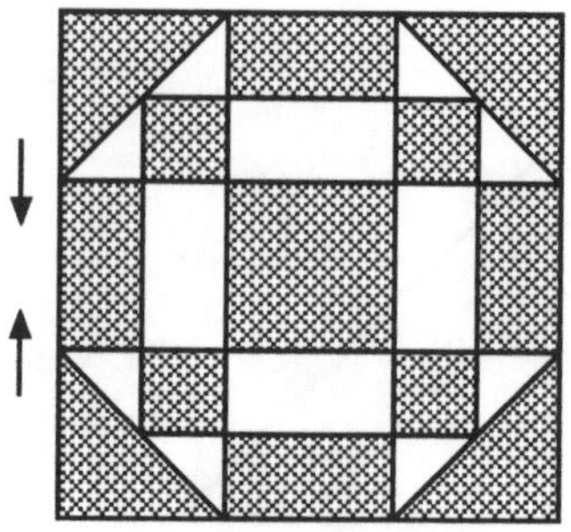   make 2

Repeat the above instructions with each pair of fabrics until you have completed all sixty blocks.

Refer to the photo on page 22 as you lay out the blocks. Use the thirty blocks which have the light backgrounds to make the center section. Arrange the blocks into six rows of five blocks. Do not sew them together yet.

Place the dark blocks around the perimeter of the quilt to give the illusion of a border. You will have four blocks left for another project or to be included in the back of your quilt.

Now, sew the quilt together by piecing horizontal rows. Press the seam allowances of the odd rows to the left. Press the seam allowances of the even rows to the right. Sew the rows together. Press the seam allowances to one side.

Options to Consider

Queen Size

Making a queen size with this light and dark placement is not recommended. This pattern results in equal numbers of light and dark (positive and negative) blocks. A queen size in this layout would use thirty-eight dark (border blocks) and seventy-two light blocks, far from equal numbers.

An optional setting idea is to place the blocks alternating the lights and darks as shown on page 70. Use twenty-three light and twenty-three dark fat quarters to make ninety blocks. Add 8" to 10" wide borders (2 3/4 yards) to finish.

Add a Narrow Inner Border

Add a narrow (cut 2" wide) border of a dark fabric before adding the outer perimeter of blocks as shown on the next page. This inner border gives an even stronger border effect to the quilt. Notice that four 2" x 9 1/2" rectangles of the narrow border fabric are used to make the top and bottom rows fit the quilt.

The quilt shown below uses only forty-eight blocks. This size and layout uses equal numbers of light background blocks and dark background blocks, leaving you without any extras. For this version you need twelve light and twelve dark fat quarters. The finished quilt is 57" x 75", a lap size. With a border added to the outer edges you could make this one fit a twin size bed. Cut the border 6" wide.

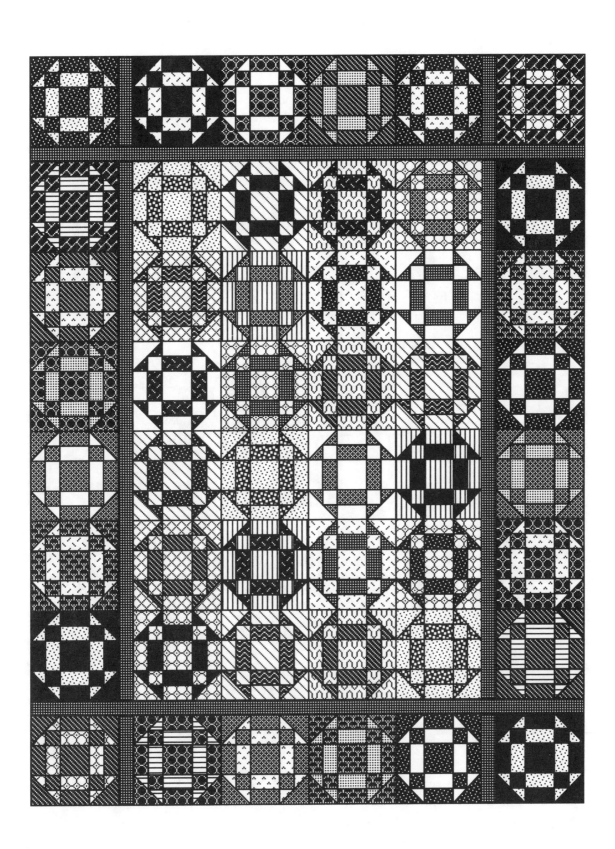

Queen Size Layout

Alternating Light and Dark Blocks

There is only one light fabric used in the illustration below to make it easier to see the pattern layout. Using a control background fabric is another option for your quilt. To determine how much background fabric is needed, divide the number of fat quarters by four. That will tell you how many yards. Round the number of yards up to the nearest half yard. See the example below.

The queen size requires 23 light fat quarters.
23 divided by 4 = 5 3/4
Purchase 6 yards.
Cut the background fabric into fat quarters and use them to cut the light fabric as directed.

Scrappy & Sensational

The size of the quilt shown on page 23 is 73" x 91", a generous twin size. With 10" borders it will fit a full size bed.

Fabric Requirements

Sixteen Fat Quarters	
Background Fabric	**4 yards**
Outer Border	**2 1/2 yards***

*This amount of fabric will allow for borders up to 10" wide.

Binding	**7/8 yard**
Backing	**5 1/2 yards****

**Buy 7 3/4 yards if you are adding 10" borders.

Cutting

Fat Quarters

Stack the fat quarters as directed in the general directions. Make two stacks of eight fabrics.

Cut off the selvages and cut strips *parallel to* the selvages as shown in figure 1.

Cut one strip 7 1/4" wide from each fabric.
  From this strip cut a total of two 7 1/4" squares of each fabric.
    Cut these squares twice, diagonally, to make four quarter-square triangles
    from each square.   Yield: 8 triangles of each fabric

Cut one strip 4 1/4" wide from each fabric.
  From this strip cut a total of four 4 1/4" squares of each fabric. If your fat quarter is too small to cut four squares, cut a fourth 2" wide strip. This strip will be used later to cut the pieces that you are lacking.

Cut three strips 2" wide from each fabric.

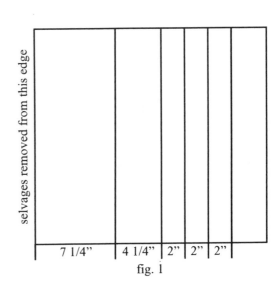

fig. 1

Background Fabric

The strips of background fabric are cut across the width of the fabric making them approximately 42" long with selvages on both of the short ends.

Cut seven strips 7 1/4" wide.

    From these strips cut a total of thirty-two 7 1/4" squares.

        Cut these squares twice, diagonally, to make four quarter-square triangles from each square.

Yield: 128 triangles

Cut seven strips 4 1/4" wide.

    From these strips cut a total of sixty-four 4 1/4" squares.

Cut nineteen strips 2" wide.

    Use these strips to cut the trapezoids as directed on the following page.

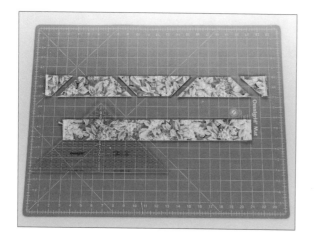

photo 14

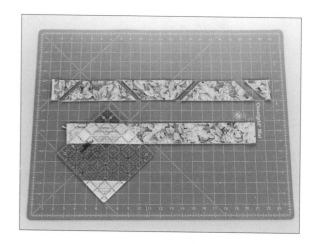

photo 15

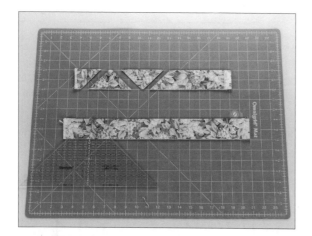

photo 16

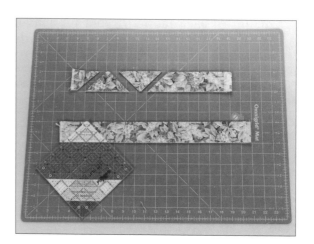

photo 17

Cutting the Trapezoids

Be conservative when you place the triangle tool or template on the 2" strips. Place them as far to the end as possible to make sure you have enough fabric to cut three trapezoids from each strip.

Lay a stack of 2" wide strips of fat quarter fabrics on your cutting mat. Use Template A on the following page or use an Omnigrid 98 or 98L triangle tool to cut trapezoids from the strips. See photo 14 on the previous page if you are using the Omnigrid 98 or 98L. Align the 6" line with the long edge of the strip. The 6" line is the line under the number six. You may want to lay the tool on the template to be sure you are using the correct line.

If you are using the template, tape it to the underside of the square corner of any ruler to make your own custom rotary cutting tool (photo 15 on the previous page).

Continue cutting trapezoids from the 2" wide strips of fat quarter fabrics until you have cut eight trapezoids from each fabric.

Cut 128 trapezoids of background fabric from the 2" wide strips using the template or the 6" line on the Omnigrid 98 or 98L tool.

If you were short when cutting the 4 1/4" squares from the fat quarter fabrics, cut four quarter-square triangles from the fourth 2" wide strip that you cut. Use either Template B on the next page or the 3" line on the Omnigrid 98 or 98L tool. See photos 16 and 17 on the previous page.

Piecing

Sew a background fabric trapezoid to the long side of each large quarter-square triangle of fat quarter fabrics. Sew a fat quarter fabric trapezoid to each of the large quarter-square triangles of background fabric. Press the seam allowances toward the fat quarter fabrics.

make 128

make 128

Sew the units from above into pairs. Pair two units of the same fabric combination. *Do not make any reverse sections. All finished sections should look like the one shown below.* Press the seam allowances in the direction shown by the arrow. *Pay attention!* It is probably opposite from the way you may expect them to be pressed.

make 128

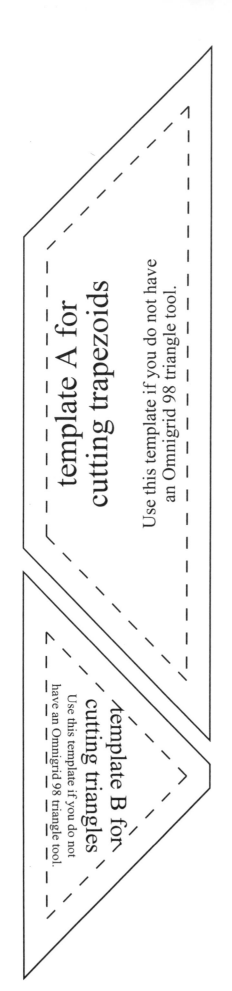

template A for
cutting trapezoids

Use this template if you do not have
an Omnigrid 98 triangle tool.

template B for
cutting triangles

Use this template if you do not
have an Omnigrid 98 triangle tool.

If you are lacking some of the 4 1/4" squares needed for the following step, use what you have and the rest of the pieces will be made later.

Place each 4 1/4" square of background fabric on a 4 1/4" square of fat quarter fabric, right sides together. Cut the pairs of squares once, diagonally, to make two pairs of half-square triangles from each.*

* If you prefer, draw the diagonal line and stitch the pairs together 1/4" away along both sides of the drawn line before cutting the diagonal. See page 41 for more instruction on these two suggested methods for constructing half-square triangle units.

Sew the pairs of triangles into half-square triangle units. Press the seam allowances toward the fat quarter fabric. Trim the dog ears.

make 128

Cut each of the half-square triangle units once, diagonally, to make A and B units. See below.

128 "A" units
8 of each fat qtr.

128 "B" units
8 of each fat qtr.

Now, *if you were short on some of your 4 1/4" squares from the fat quarters and you cut quarter-square triangles from an extra 2" strip*, cut your remaining 4 1/4" squares of background fabric into quarter-square triangles. Use the quarter-square triangles of fat quarter fabric and background fabric to make A and B units. Be sure to make two of A and two of B from each fat quarter fabric. When you have finished there should be a total of 128 units of A and 128 units of B, eight of each fat quarter fabric.

Cut your remaining
4 1/4" squares of
background into
quarter-square
triangles.

Sew the A units to the large triangle/trapezoid sections. Press the seam allowances toward the A's. See below, left. Again, use only one fat quarter fabric in each block.

Sew the sections from above into pairs. Press the seam allowances to one side. See below, center.

Add the B's to the blocks. Press the seam allowances toward the B's. See below, right. *NOTE: **The seam allowances will not oppose each other when adding one of the B's to the block.** Pin this seam to match it. Do not press it in the opposite direction. That will keep all of the seam allowances pressed in the correct directions for completing the quilt top.*

Arrange the blocks into nine rows of seven blocks. There will be one leftover block. Refer to the photo on page 23. ***Notice that every other block is rotated a quarter turn so that the corners come together to make a pinwheel.*** Sew the blocks into horizontal rows. Press the seam allowances of the odd rows to the left. Press the seam allowances of the even rows to the right. Sew the rows together. Press the seam allowances to one side.

Add borders with overlapped corners. To complete the quilt as shown, cut the borders 6" wide. However, there is enough fabric to cut wider borders, up to 10" wide. See page 10 for more instruction on borders.

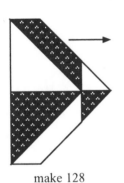

make 128

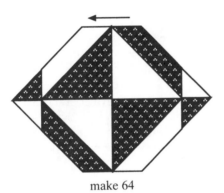

make 64

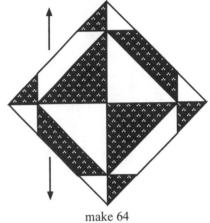

make 64

Options to Consider

Queen Size

A queen size quilt will require seventy-two blocks (eight blocks per row/nine rows). The quilt will measure 90" x 99" with the addition of 9" wide borders. Cut them 9 1/2" wide.

With the same fabric placement as the full size version you will need the following to complete a queen size quilt top:

Fabric	Amount
fat quarters	18 fat quarters
background	4 1/2 yards
border	2 3/4 yards

Scrappy Background

Replace the background fabric with light fat quarters. Use the same number of light fat quarters as dark fat quarters. Cut the light fat quarters exactly as you cut the dark fat quarters.

Random Fabric Placement

Instead of making blocks with only two fabrics in them, use the fabrics randomly, being sure to place light fabrics and dark fabrics in their respective positions to create the overall pattern. This random placement works well whether you use one background fabric or many.

About the Author

Debbie Caffrey is a self-published author of seven books and eleven patterns. In addition, she has designed and published over one hundred patterns in a frequently changing line of mystery quilts. She has taught many energy-filled workshops nationwide for guilds and shops. Some of the past venues include Houston Quilt Festival, Minnesota Quilters' Conference, Festival of Classes in Bend, Oregon, and the Road to California. Debbie has contributed seven articles to *Traditional Quiltworks* magazine and has appeared on two episodes of HGTV's television program, *Simply Quilts*.

Debbie and her husband Dan returned to New Mexico in the fall of 2000 where they live near Santa Fe. They had lived in Anchorage, Alaska, since 1979 where they raised their children Monica, Erin, and Mark. Besides quilting, Debbie enjoys long walks and drives and experiencing new places. In New Mexico Debbie and Dan spend many hours exploring the back roads and trails, watching the birds and animals, and studying the plants, rocks, and vistas of the Southwest.

Other Books by Debbie Caffrey

Noodle Soup
Open a Can of Worms
Quilting Season
Scraps to You, Too
~~*Blocks and Quilts Everywhere!*~~ Sorry, this one is out of print.
An Alaskan Sampler

Please visit us on the web.
www.debbiescreativemoments.com